LIVING FROM

THE HEART

LIVING FROM THE HEART

Nirmala

Endless Satsang Foundation

This book consists of three related teachings about the Heart by Nirmala. The poetry is from *Gifts with No Giver* by Nirmala.

Endless Satsang Foundation

www.endless-satsang.com

nirmalanow@aol.com

ISBN: 978-1-4382-5863-8

CONTENTS

What Is the Truth?—The Heart's Capacity to Show You the Truth—The Heart's Quickness—The Role of Judgments—Positive Judgment—All Truth Is Relative—Your Perfect Wisdom—Applying Your Heart's Wisdom—The Many Sizes of Truth—The Deeper Currents of Thought—The Thought

That You Are the Body—The Sense of *Me*—There Is Only Love—True Freedom—Who Are You?

You Are the Source—Just One Being—You Can't Run out of Love—Loving Through the Senses—Loving Beyond the Senses—Love Reveals Inner Beauty—Beyond the Experience of Love

INTRODUCTION

For centuries, spiritual teachings have pointed us to the Heart as the source of wisdom, truth, peace, and love. We call it the Heart because these deeper realities are experienced most strongly in the region of the physical heart. However, the spiritual Heart is not limited to a location in your body. The Heart is the totality of your connection with the essential qualities and greater dimensions of your true nature as limitless Being. Any full exploration of the larger truth of your Being must include a discovery of the capacities and qualities of this tender, loving, and wise aspect of your true nature.

This book consists of three related pieces that explore living from the spiritual Heart. Part One, *From the Heart*, offers simple ways to drop your awareness into the Heart and thereby shift into a more open, allowing perspective, and to more fully experience the world and your true nature as aware space. It goes on to explore dropping awareness into the belly and ultimately into the larger spiritual Heart, which includes the mind, heart and belly. These simple shifts in perspective can profoundly alter your experience of life and its challenges. It turns out it doesn't matter what you experience, what matters is where you experience it from.

Part Two, *The Heart's Wisdom*, explains how the Heart is a wise and accurate guide to the truth. The truth is whatever opens your Heart and quiets your mind. This simple definition cuts through any confusing ideas and beliefs to the direct source of wisdom and guidance available in your own Heart.

Part Three, *Love Is for Giving*, points to the true source of love in your own Heart. The essence of love is the spacious, open attention of our awareness. Awareness is the gentlest, kindest, and most intimate force in the world. It touches everything but doesn't impose or make demands. Surprisingly, this awareness, or love, is experienced most fully when you give it to others, not when you get it from others. The more love you give, the more love you experience. It is by freely giving love that we are filled with love.

Throughout, there is a pointing beyond the experience of the Heart and its wisdom, peace, and love to the possibility of recognizing these essential qualities as who and what you are. The Heart with all its joy, satisfaction, peace, love, and wisdom is not just something you can experience more fully; it is what you have always been and always will be. In recognizing your true nature as this fullness of Being, you can ultimately rest from all seeking and effort, and just be who you are.

PART 1

From the Heart

Dropping out of Your Mind and into Your Being

CHAPTER 1

We Are All Baby Ducks

You may think it matters what happens. But what if the only thing that matters is where you are experiencing from, where you are looking from? What if you could experience all of life from a spacious, open perspective where anything can happen and there is room for all of it, where there is no need to pick and choose, to put up barriers or resist any of it, where nothing is a problem and everything just adds to the richness of life? What if this open, spacious perspective was the most natural and easy thing to do?

It may sound too good to be true, but we all have a natural capacity to experience life this way. The only requirement is to look from the Heart, not just figuratively, but to look from the subtle energetic center located in the center of the chest instead of looking out from the eyes and the head—and not just to look, but to listen, feel, and sense from the Heart.

In some spiritual traditions we are encouraged to look in the Heart, and yet what does that mean exactly? Often we are so used to looking and sensing through the head and the mind that when we are asked to look in the Heart, we look *through* the head into the Heart to see what is there. Usually we end up just thinking about the Heart. But what if you could drop into the Heart and look from there? How would your life look right now? Is it possible that there is another world right in front of you that you can only see with the Heart and not with the mind?

In what follows, you are invited to explore this radically different perspective and to find out what is true and real when the world and your life are viewed from the Heart of Being. It may both delight and shock you to find that so much richness, wonder, and beauty lie so close and are so immediately available to you. But don't take my word for it. See for yourself if your experience fits with this simple, yet profound, way to shift in awareness to a more complete view of your life, your world, and ultimately your true nature as that openness, wonder, and beauty.

As an aside, some people are more visual, some are more auditory, and some are more in touch with feelings or physical sensations. One or two of these modes are referred to in the exercises that follow. Feel free to translate and use whatever mode is most natural to you. For instance, you might find it easier to listen with your head or Heart rather than look from your head or Heart. You may want to experiment with the other senses also.

YOUR NATURE AS AWARENESS

Right now as you read these words, who or what are you really? Are you the body, mind, and personality? Or are you the spacious awareness or aware space that these appear in? What you are is this space. It is a remarkable space that is alive and aware. You could say this is what you are made of: You are aware space.

> **Exercise:** *Take a moment to sense behind your eyes. Turn your attention to the space behind your eyes. What do you sense there? If you only refer to your experience in this moment, what do you find in the space behind your eyes? Does this space have a capacity to experience sensation? Is there awareness in the space behind your eyes? Don't worry for now what this awareness is like or what you are aware of. Simply check if you are aware of anything right now, anything at all. If you let go of any ideas about what awareness is supposed to be like or what is supposed to happen in awareness, then you can begin to explore this simple miracle of awareness going on behind your eyes.*

That aware space is the real you. It is what you are made of, what you exist as here and now. It also turns out that everything that really matters in life is found in this aware space. This is where love, peace, joy, compassion, wisdom, strength, and a sense of worth are found. These are qualities of your true nature as aware space. These are qualities of the real you. Everything you might ever need, including everything you need to know, is to be found in that spacious presence behind your eyes.

I invite you to play in this spacious awareness. If you wanted to find out about the nature of water, it would be helpful to play in it whenever you had a chance. So if you want to find out about this aware presence that you are, you might want to explore along as we splash around in the space of awareness.

One bit of good news: It doesn't matter at all for the purposes of our exploration what you are aware of. It doesn't matter what you are experiencing. It doesn't matter if you are happy or sad, healthy or sick, rich or poor, enlightened or suffering, expanded or contracted. However, the only place you can play in awareness is where awareness is right now. So as you explore the awareness, you need to refer to whatever is happening right now... and now... and now because that is where awareness is found.

HOW AWARENESS IS IMPRINTED

Realizing your true nature as awareness would be incredibly simple except for one thing: This awareness that you are can be shaped. Just like water takes on the shape of the container you pour it into, the awareness that you are is shaped by your thoughts, feelings, desires, hopes, dreams, worries, sensations, and experiences. It is shaped by everything that happens. Sometimes this shaping is so strong that it seems the awareness has gotten very small and that you have gotten very small. This is not really a problem as the awareness itself is not harmed, and it can always expand again.

This awareness is not only temporarily shaped by experience, but can become imprinted onto an experience or an object in awareness. You may have heard of how baby ducks become imprinted in the first few hours of their lives: They will follow whatever or whomever they are first aware of, usually the mother duck. However, they can also be imprinted on anything, including a scientist who is studying them, in which case, they will follow the scientist around.

There is nothing wrong with this; it helps baby ducks survive in the wild to follow their mother wherever she goes. It is an inherent capacity of all awareness to become imprinted, or conditioned, in this way. Every time an experience leaves a lasting impression in your awareness, you have been imprinted or conditioned by that experience.

However for humans, this imprinting is more complicated than for ducks. You can be imprinted onto many different things. One of the things you are most imprinted on is your body. You are so strongly imprinted onto your body that most of the time, your awareness follows your body wherever it goes—just like a baby duck follows its mother. Check it out: Get up and walk into another room. Does your awareness stay in the room you just left or follow your body into the other room? We are all baby ducks when it comes to our bodies.

Another thing you are profoundly imprinted on is your own mind or thoughts (from here on when thoughts are mentioned, it will refer to the entire range of internal experience: thoughts, beliefs, feelings, desires, hopes, fantasies, etc.). So when a thought, a fear, or a longing arises, your awareness flows to that. Check it out: When you stop thinking one thought and begin thinking another, does your awareness stay on the original thought? Or does it follow your thoughts wherever they go? Isn't it kind of like a baby duck following its momma across the pond, out onto the meadow and into a creek?

You have been imprinted onto your physical body and your mind. This isn't bad. Just as with baby ducks, it has some benefits for your survival, although not always: Just as a baby duck will follow its mother onto a busy freeway, your awareness will follow your thoughts into all kinds of silly and sometimes dangerous places.

Since you are almost always aware of your body and your mind (because awareness follows your body and mind around), you come to the mistaken conclusion that you *are* your body and your mind. You fail to recognize that what you are is the empty, spacious awareness that the body and mind appear in. You assume, since they are almost always here, *I am the body and the mind.*

This is a simple and completely understandable mistake. Unfortunately, it is also a colossal mistake and the source of all your suffering. It's as if you had a fly on your nose that stuck around so long that you decided you were the fly. Imagine how confused you would feel and act if you believed you were a fly. You would spend all day eating rotten food and trying to mate with other flies!

Well you are making as big a mistake when you conclude that you are the body and the mind. It's not that there is anything wrong with the body or the mind; it's just that they are not really who you are. All the problems you experience are only problems for the body or the mind. The spacious awareness has no problems. How can space have a problem? It can't be harmed or diminished in any way. You can set off a bomb in space, and when the dust settles, the space will be completely unharmed.

This mistaken identity as the body and mind creates all of your suffering. If the body or mind were having an experience that you considered a problem, but you realized that you were not the body or the mind, would you suffer from those problems? Right now, are you suffering dramatically over the problems of someone you have never met? Probably not, since they aren't your problems. So what if none of your problems are really *your* problems? What if the spacious awareness that you really are can't have problems?

> **Exercise:** *Consider for a moment something you are experiencing that seems like a problem. Without changing your experience or even your knowledge and understanding of the problem in any way, check if the space in which the thoughts or circumstances of the problem are happening has any difficulty with those thoughts and circumstances. Does the space in which the difficulty is appearing have a problem? Can space itself ever have a problem? If for just a moment, you identify with the space that both you and the problem are in, do you have a problem? Can you as the space ever have a problem?*

Recognizing yourself as aware space is a radical shift in your usual identity or sense of yourself. It may be a while before you can really believe or, more importantly, consistently experience your identity as aware space. We are profoundly conditioned or imprinted onto our usual identification with the body and mind. You may discover you have a deep and abiding conviction that you really are the body and your inner life of thoughts and feelings. We don't give up our deepest convictions easily.

As you read this, you might want to hold open the possibility that you are mistaken. Try out the possibility that you really are the space, and see for yourself if this fits more with the evidence of your experience. If you can temporarily set aside the conviction that who you are is your physical body and the flow of mental activity, you will be better able to sense for yourself the truth being pointed to here.

WHAT IT IS LIKE TO LOOK OUT FROM THE HEAD

As you were growing up and everyone was teaching and conditioning you to follow the experience of your body and mind, your identity moved into the body and head. Since your eyes, ears, nose, taste buds, and brain are all located in your head, the awareness and the identity also became localized there. Since the head is where your awareness became located, that is where you now look, feel, and sense from.

As a result of awareness flowing through your head, it becomes shaped by your thoughts. This wouldn't matter if you only had a thought occasionally, but most of us have very busy minds. As a result, awareness is profoundly shaped and limited by its tendency to flow through the head. Every little thought that arises takes your awareness for a ride through inner landscapes of doubt, worry, hope, and conjecture.

Most of the time these inner landscapes have only a slight correspondence with what is really happening, and often they have absolutely nothing to do with reality. Have you ever thought someone was mad at you, only to find out he or she just had a stomach ache? So why do we pay so much attention to our thoughts? Because every now and then, they are right. Every now and then, a thought does correspond to something out there. As any psychology student knows, an intermittent reward, or success, is more powerfully reinforcing than a constant one.

So you end up with your awareness flowing through your head and through your thoughts. What is awareness like when it flows through thoughts? What effect do your thoughts have on awareness itself?

Thought itself is a very small phenomenon. All of your thoughts fit between your ears, so how big can they be? So when awareness flows through thoughts, it becomes very small. Consequently, your sense of self becomes small because fundamentally you are the awareness. So when awareness contracts onto a thought, it takes on the size and shape of that experience.

However, when awareness gets focused onto something it also magnifies it. Try it out: Pick up an object and focus all your attention on it. Does it appear smaller or bigger when you focus on it? It tends to look bigger. When you habitually focus on your thoughts, the content or meaning of them is magnified, even as your awareness and the sense of self is contracted. When your awareness is flowing so constantly to your thoughts and through the head, your awareness becomes chronically narrowed and limited.

This is not bad and even has some value at times for survival, but it is also limiting and narrow. When your awareness is narrow and limited, you miss a lot of what is happening. Much of reality is simply not noticed because when awareness is contracted, unawareness is expanded.

Exercise: *For a moment, put your hands around your eyes like a set of blinders. Does your awareness of the room you are in get bigger or smaller? The room doesn't get smaller, but your awareness of it shrinks— you are seeing less of the room. Now notice: Does the part of the room that you aren't seeing get bigger or smaller? Of course what you aren't seeing gets bigger if you are seeing less.*

The net effect of being imprinted onto your body and especially onto your head and your thoughts is that you tend to look out from your head: You live in your head and look out from it. You see, smell, hear, feel, sense, and ponder life with your head. That means that what you are seeing, smelling, hearing, sensing, and pondering is limited by and filtered through your thoughts. Your thoughts mediate between you and reality and interfere with seeing it more fully and purely. They color it, change it, and include only part of it. In a sense, you are living in a dream, all because you are looking out of your head and your thoughts.

This is so common that you don't even notice that this shaping of awareness is occurring. You get used to it. Just as you assume that the body and mind must be what you are because they are always present, you also assume the world you see through your mind is the real world. You assume that things really are the way your mind perceives them.

While it may be difficult to distinguish the effects of this imprinting, you may be able to sense how typically narrow or tight or contracted your perspective is. Because of the magnifying effect of this narrow perspective, the content of your thoughts can seem quite huge and even overwhelming. This is how you make a mountain out of a molehill. For a moment, see if you can sense directly the shape of the awareness in this moment—not the content of your thoughts— but the flow of awareness itself.

Exercise: *Awareness is flowing in this moment. Just check, are you aware of anything at all? Really anything at all will do for this exercise, including a thought arising in your mind or simply the words* *appearing on this page. So if you are aware of something right now, where is this awareness flowing from? Can you sense where the awareness is coming from? Is it coming from your big toe, the ceiling, or does it seem to be coming from your head?*

What is the awareness itself like in this moment? Is it expanded, open, and flowing freely, or is it more focused and narrow? There is no right answer, and awareness is always subtly changing, becoming narrower or more open. What is awareness like right now, not the content of your experience, but the experiencing itself? It may be the usual awareness that is shaped by flowing through your head, but just notice what that is like.

Awareness that is shaped by flowing through the head and by thoughts is typically tight and constricted. Just as a muscle requires effort to stay contracted, this tightness of awareness has an effortful quality. It is often not very satisfying, like trying to drink through a very narrow straw. You can never quite get enough of what is happening, so naturally you try harder: You think harder and try to understand what is happening, which only narrows the view even more.

Awareness that flows through your mind creates an underlying sense of there not being enough. Even if you are having a wonderful experience, there is a sense of not being able to absorb it all, so you may want to hang on to it or try to capture it some way (e.g., in a snapshot or home video) so that later you can get more of the experience. This is all the result of looking through your head. It is so habitual that it seems normal to feel so dissatisfied and incomplete.

But what if there is another way of looking that shapes the world in a completely different way—so differently that the world doesn't even appear to be the same world? What would it be like to look from your Heart?

CHAPTER 2

Another Way to Sense Your World

THE FLEXIBILITY OF PERSPECTIVE

Despite the habitual tendency to look out from your head, it is actually quite simple to move the point where your perspective originates from. Some have suggested that dyslexics have an unusually flexible perspective that moves so freely that, in a sense, they can see words on a page from both the front and back. As a result, they can see letters in their usual order and also from the opposite side, which makes them appear backwards. For a dyslexic, there are benefits to learning to stabilize, or fix, their perspective, where they look from.

However, for the rest of us, moving our perspective around can free it up. In many of the therapeutic interventions used in Neuro-Linguistic Programming, a person is invited to see himself or herself from the outside. This gives a unique, and often useful, perspective on what is happening.

Without moving the perspective outside the body but simply down into the Heart, you can profoundly alter the shaping of your awareness.

THE SHIFT INTO THE HEART

The center of your chest, which is next to your physical heart, is often considered the spiritual center of your Being. For many centuries, it was believed that thinking happened in the heart rather than in the brain. What would it be like to experience the world from this energetic center instead of from the head? What effect would that have on your experience of the world and of yourself?

> **Exercise:** *Try this exercise first with your eyes closed and then open. Notice what you are aware of in this moment: the sounds, a thought, the objects around you. Notice if you are looking or listening or sensing from the head, and notice what that is like. Now gently drop your sensing down into your Heart. This is not a matter of sensing the Heart or feeling what is in your Heart, but feeling your surroundings from the center of your chest. At first, it can be helpful to rest your hand on the center of your chest next to your heart, to help orient*

yourself to looking from this place. Allow what you are seeing to be seen by your Heart instead of your head. What is it like to sense, listen, and look from your Heart? Pick an object and sense it with your Heart instead of your head. How is that?

The key is to allow awareness to flow from the Heart. Especially at first, it's not important to sense the Heart itself. It's simpler at first if you just sense an ordinary object, like a piece of furniture, *from* your Heart. The important thing is where your awareness seems to be located. Because of the strongly imprinted tendency to look from the head and through your thoughts, you may find at first that you are looking *into* your Heart, or you may be *thinking* about what it would be like to look from the Heart. If you are just imagining what that would be like, your awareness would still be shaped by thoughts—in this case, a thought about this new way of looking.

See if you can do this, if only for a moment—just look or sense from your Heart. What is that like even if it only lasts briefly? Does your awareness open up and expand? Do you sense things in a different way? Most people find that their awareness becomes softer, wider, and more open. This is simply the way awareness flows when it's not being so narrowly shaped by the mind. Just as a muscle naturally expands when you aren't contracting it, awareness expands when it's not being shaped and constricted by your thoughts.

> **Exercise:** *Take some time to play with this new way of sensing and looking. What do the objects around you look or feel like when you look at them from the Heart? How do you experience other people with your Heart? What are sounds or music like when you listen from the Heart? What about your thoughts? They may still be arising in the usual way, but what if you listen to and watch them from the Heart? Do they seem as important, or are they just passing words and pictures in a large open space? See how the world looks and feels from here. It is another world. Explore this new world. Discover what your day-to-day experiences are like when they are sensed from the Heart.*

As mentioned, it can be helpful to close your eyes at first when sensing from the Heart. Because the eyes are located in the head, when you are seeing, the tendency is for awareness to locate itself in the head rather than in the Heart. So until you get the hang of *looking* from your Heart, it might be easier to simply *sense* objects and people with your Heart with your eyes closed. Then slowly add listening and, finally, looking with your eyes open.

Keep checking to notice if the awareness is actually flowing from the Heart or if it has moved back up into your head. If it does, that's fine—no harm is done to the awareness. But when it does shift back into the more habitual perspective of looking from the head, notice what that is like. Does it stay open and expanded, or does it become narrow and focused, like a magnifying glass or a microscope? Then you can gently move the perspective back down to the Heart and check for yourself what that's like. Does the awareness open up again and relax?

At first, there may be so much momentum to looking from the head that you may only be able to sense or look from the Heart for a few seconds at a time. That's fine. Just notice what you can about the quality of your awareness whenever it is actually in your Heart. With time, you should be able to extend the time you listen, look, or sense from your Heart. Maybe you will find you can listen to an entire song from your Heart or watch a sunset from your Heart. What if you were to watch TV, wash the dishes, or talk on the phone while looking and listening from the Heart? You may find yourself thinking about your life or planning your weekend, but for a change, notice these thoughts from your Heart.

Your awareness can flow from more than one place at a time. At times, it may be flowing mostly from your head, and at other times, mostly from your Heart. If the awareness is flowing partly from your head and partly from your Heart, the qualities of the awareness will be somewhere in between. It might be more open and allowing than usual, but still have a degree of focus and direction.

THE QUALITIES OF THE HEART'S PERSPECTIVE

Here are some clues that awareness is flowing at least partly from the Heart: The awareness will be wider and more open, the boundaries between the awareness and the objects in awareness will seem less substantial, there will be more of a sense of oneness and connection with whatever you are sensing, and thoughts will be of less concern or not noticed at all. When something is very small, it can be easily overlooked, and thoughts are actually very small realities.

Most of the time, you experience thoughts from the head. This is like having your nose up close to a TV screen. The content of your thoughts is right in front of your awareness. When you drop into the Heart, thoughts continue to occur, but you will be experiencing them from down in the Heart. Now it is as if that TV is playing up in the attic instead of right in front of you. This puts the content of your thoughts into perspective. When experienced from the Heart, they are not such a big deal.

When awareness is flowing through the Heart, it also includes much more of what is happening. As a result, the experience is much more satisfying. Instead of trying to take life in through a narrow view, you can drink to your Heart's content. There is a richness and fullness to even very ordinary experiences.

If the opposite qualities are predominant, that would mean you have returned to looking from your head. So if the view contracts, the boundaries seem more real, you feel separate or dissatisfied, and thoughts suddenly take up the entire screen of your consciousness, chances are you (as awareness) are residing in the head again.

Exercise: *Pick something in your environment and then sense it first with your head and then with your Heart. How are these different? The contrast between the two modes of looking, listening, and sensing will allow you to notice the differences in the awareness itself as it flows from the head and then from the Heart. For this exercise, keep your awareness on the same object, sound, or thought. Then any difference will be directly related to where you are sensing, listening, or looking from and not due to experiencing something different in your environment.*

FEELINGS AND EMOTIONS

What about the emotions that might arise in the area of your heart? Just as with thoughts or objects in your environment, what matters in terms of your emotions is where you are sensing them from. You can use your Heart to sense, look, and listen to any feelings that may arise and be felt in the heart area.

> **Exercise:** *Notice the emotional quality in your heart area right now. Whether it is quite neutral or strongly emotional, just note what that is. What happens if you experience it from the Heart itself? Does that give the emotion more space to expand and flow? Is it as big a deal? Looking from the Heart allows awareness to flow from a deeper place in your Being, deeper than your emotions and desires. Allow the awareness to flow from this deeper place to the unfolding experience of your emotions.*

THE CONTENTS OF THE HEAD

What about thoughts? What happens to your thoughts when you look or listen from the Heart? Thoughts are just activity in the mind, and yet you can hear, see, or feel this activity much in the same way you hear, see, and feel the physical world. However this activity is all in your mind; it is not even as substantial as the smallest physical object. Thoughts are actually a very small phenomenon.

Have you ever blocked your view of the moon with just your thumb? Because your thumb is so close, it can block out a much larger object that is far away. Similarly, when you are looking or listening from your head, your thoughts are right there—up close and right in front of you. As a result, they tend to block your view of everything else.

Imagine walking around all day with a TV hanging right in front of your nose. You might have a tendency to not see and hear much else than the pictures and sounds on the television. Likewise, when you look from your head, you mostly see your thoughts. Furthermore, the content of your thoughts is magnified because the awareness is so narrowly focused when it flows through your head. You watch the television of your mind through a magnifying glass. No wonder we become so engrossed in our thoughts.

Looking through your head and through your thoughts is a drastically limited view of reality, and the content of your thoughts is often not so pretty. The mind is full of judgments, fears, doubts, and worries. It is filled with negative voices and pictures of what could go wrong. Experiencing life through the busy mind is often unpleasant. Even when your thoughts are positive, they aren't necessarily what is really happening, and reality can be disappointing when it doesn't match your positive fantasies.

The good news is that it doesn't matter so much what you are experiencing. What matters is where you are experiencing it from.

Exercise: *Notice your thoughts as they arise moment to moment. Now notice where you are noticing them from. If you are listening, watching, and sensing your thoughts from the head, what is that like? How big do they look, sound, or feel? How important do they seem? Now without changing your thoughts in any way, allow your awareness to flow to them from your Heart. What is that like? How big do they look, sound, or feel up there in the head from way down in the chest? How important do they seem now?*

Because the view from the Heart is so wide and inclusive, something relatively small like a thought, belief, memory, fantasy, or idea can be recognized as small. The content of your thoughts may or may not change, but your thoughts won't take up so much of the screen of consciousness when awareness includes much more. Thoughts can be experienced as something relatively small, like a bug walking next to the Grand Canyon. Relative to thoughts, the world is a big and limitless place. When you experience your thoughts from the Heart, your thoughts shrink down to actual size.

Have you ever tried to quiet your thoughts? Usually you just end up thinking about thinking less. But you can quiet the impact of your thoughts in an instant by simply allowing the awareness of them to flow from your Heart. At times the thoughts will drop right out of awareness. When the experience of the rest of reality is so full and complete, you don't notice the thoughts, although they continue to occur. The experience is like first seeing the ocean or the Grand Canyon: Your mind falls silent because you are too busy taking in the vastness to notice your thoughts. Similarly, the present moment and its many dimensions can be an experience even vaster than the ocean when you are experiencing it through your Heart.

Exercise: *Allow your awareness to flow from your Heart to everything you are experiencing in this moment. Unlike the mind, which can only think about one thing at a time, awareness flowing through the Heart can take in an infinite number of sensations, thoughts, sights, sounds, and subtle energies. With awareness flowing from your Heart, notice what you are seeing, hearing, and sensing in your body. Now also include the flow of thoughts, feelings, and impulses. Add in all of the subtle or energetic ways of sensing you are capable of. Include the simple presence of limitless space and time. Allow awareness to flow to all of these and more simultaneously. As long as your awareness is flowing mostly through your Heart, you will find you can include much more in awareness than usual.*

RESTING IN THE HEART

In many spiritual traditions, the Heart is recognized as the true center of Being. In the way we are exploring it here, you could also say that the Heart doesn't shape or limit the flow of awareness as much as the head. As a result, you can experience your Being more fully when awareness is flowing through the Heart. Just as you can experience more of the nature of water by immersing yourself in it rather than just experiencing a drop of it, the experience of Being is much more dramatic and obvious when awareness is located in the Heart than in the head.

As you play more with this possibility of looking from the Heart, you may find that the Heart becomes a familiar and comfortable place for awareness to rest. While awareness through the head is effortful because of the contraction of awareness, when that same awareness flows through the Heart, relaxation and expansion naturally occurs. The awareness can spread out, expand, and simply rest from all the effort of focusing and figuring things out.

Spiritual books and teachers often suggest resting in the Heart. However, if you are looking into the Heart from the head, it's not so easy to rest there. It can seem effortful to keep that narrow focus of awareness on the Heart. But if you allow awareness to flow from the Heart, then it instantly becomes easy to also rest in the Heart. There is no effort required. The

Heart is where you reside in those moments, and you can only rest right where you are in the moment.

> **Exercise:** *Allow your awareness to flow from the Heart. It doesn't really matter what you are aware of, only where you are aware from. Now simply settle in. Allow yourself to rest here in the spaciousness of the Heart's perspective. From here, there is nothing to do and nowhere to go. You are Home.*

CHAPTER 3

What About the Real World?

LOOKING FROM THE BELLY

Looking from the Heart adds richness to experience and opens up whole new dimensions to daily life, and yet often there is resistance to truly resting in the Heart. It can seem impractical or too vulnerable to consistently view the world in such an expanded, open, uncensored way. So we often return to our old habit of looking through the mind and its false sense of being in control. The mind gives us a sense that we know what is going to happen. Even thinking we know what should happen feels reassuring, even though that is irrelevant to what actually does happen.

Moving in the world while looking from the mind has tremendous drawbacks, however. Most of what you think about never does actually happen, and the tendency to focus on the mind's contents can prevent you from fully noticing what is actually happening.

When life is demanding, it is still not necessary to contract into the mind, with its many blind spots and severely limited perspective. There is another possibility, which is to look, listen, and sense the world from your belly. Just as you can allow awareness to flow from the Heart center in your chest, you can allow awareness to sink down even further and flow from a spot a few finger widths below the belly button called the *hara*.

Exercise: *Try this exercise first with your eyes closed and then open. Notice what you are aware of in this moment: the sounds, a thought, the objects around you. Notice if you are looking, listening, or sensing from the head, and notice what that is like. Now gently drop your sensing down into your belly. This isn't a matter of sensing the belly or feeling what is in the belly, but experiencing your surroundings from the belly. It can be helpful, at first, to rest your hand just below your belly button to orient you to looking, listening, and sensing from this place. Allow what you are seeing, listening, and sensing to be seen, listened, and sensed by your belly instead of your head. What is it like to sense, listen, and look from your belly? Pick an object*

*and sense it with your belly instead of with your head.
How is that?*

The belly is a reservoir of strength and capability. It has a solidity and firmness that can stand up to whatever life dishes out. When you look from the belly, the view doesn't contract and problems don't become magnified like they do when you look from the head. Instead, the view remains open and expanded. There is also a sense of something solid and real that is experiencing all of it. The real you is here and able to do whatever needs to be done.

Awareness is shaped by the belly into a solid and substantial presence that is not easily overwhelmed or even unduly influenced by circumstances. Looking from the belly is a much more effective way to move in the world than thinking. It is a place where action and consistency come naturally.

Exercise: *Take some time to play with this new way of sensing and looking. What do the objects around you look or feel like when you look from the belly? How do you experience other people with your belly? What are sounds or music like when you listen from the belly? What about your thoughts? They may still be arising, but what if you listen to and watch them from down in the belly? Do they seem important, or are they just passing words and pictures in a large open space? Do* *thoughts or circumstances have a lot of impact, or are they sensed from something that is solid and real that isn't affected much by ideas and events? See how the world looks and feels from here. It is another world. Explore this new world. Discover what your day-to-day experiences are like when they are sensed from the belly.*

The belly grounds awareness in the real world without magnifying or distorting the content of your awareness. Sensing from the belly is a direct and simple meeting of whatever happens, which includes a strong and capable sense of yourself. After all, you are part of what is here right now. Why leave out a sense of your own presence? Your existence can be included in every experience, and when you look from the belly, your existence can seem to have the presence and substance of an entire mountain of Being.

From this solid base of your Being, thoughts impinge less on your awareness. There is no need to change or quiet your thoughts. Just find out what they are like when seen from the belly.

Exercise: *Notice your thoughts as they arise moment to moment. Now notice where you are noticing them from. If you are listening, watching, and sensing them from your head, what is that like? How big do they* *look, sound, or feel? How important do they seem? Now without changing your thoughts in any way, allow your awareness to flow to them from your belly. What is that like? How big do they look, sound, or feel up in the head from way down in the lower abdomen? How important do they seem now? Do they still have the ability to unduly influence or sway you from your position in the here and now?*

Thoughts are useful when you recognize them as just thoughts. Looking from the belly can give you a sense of being a substantial presence that is not unduly influenced by passing thoughts.

You can also rest here in the belly. You can rest as a mountain of awareness and feel the stillness of that immense presence.

Exercise: *Allow your awareness to flow from the belly. It doesn't really matter what you are aware of, only where you are aware from. Now simply settle in. Allow yourself to rest here in the solidness of the belly's perspective. From here, there is nothing you need to do and nothing you can't do. You are real. You exist.*

PUTTING IT ALL TOGETHER

Looking from the Heart and looking from the belly can add so much to your awareness and to the sense of satisfaction and capacity you feel in life. Looking from the head can also be a useful capability of your awareness. Although thoughts are not in and of themselves profound realities, there is no reason to deny their existence or usefulness. It is only when you are habitually stuck in looking from the head that thoughts can limit your perspective and range of awareness in an ongoing way, but it's not necessary to limit yourself from ever looking from the mind.

Fortunately, your awareness is incredibly flexible and can move in and out of any perspective. There is no need to limit yourself to one perspective or another.

> **Exercise:** *Pick something in your environment and then continue to sense it first with your head, then with your Heart, and then with your belly. How are these three different? The contrast between the three modes of looking, listening, and sensing will allow you to notice the differences in the awareness itself as it moves up into the head, down into the Heart, and further down into the belly. For this exercise, keep your awareness on just one object, sound, or thought. Then any difference will be directly related to where you are*

looking from and not due to experiencing something different in your environment. You can repeat this exercise with several different experiences to become familiar with each mode and gain a sense of when each might be appropriate or useful.

The mind is especially appropriate when focusing and performing certain tasks, like balancing a checkbook, giving someone directions, teasing apart a philosophical idea, or memorizing a phone number.

The belly is especially appropriate when action, consistency, strength, or discrimination is needed. Examples are times when you need to persist to get something done, when you need to say no to someone, when it is important to either act or leave an uncomfortable or dangerous situation, and when an experience is especially intense or overwhelming, including overwhelmingly pleasurable.

The Heart's perspective is always appropriate, especially when the opportunity exists to simply rest and be. It is always enough to just be. This spacious awareness that you are is all you ever really need. In it, is everything that really matters in life: love, peace, wisdom, clarity, joy, strength, value, and wonder. The true Heart is much, much bigger than the space in your chest and actually includes your head, your belly, and everything else.

LOOKING FROM THE HEART, BELLY, AND MIND

This true Heart is your real home. The perspectives of the head, the chest, and the belly are all components of this spacious Heart of Being. One way to experience this is to use all three modes of perception simultaneously.

> **Exercise:** *Try this exercise first with your eyes closed and then open. Notice what you are aware of in this moment: the sounds, a thought, the objects around you. Notice if you are looking, listening, or sensing from the head, and notice what that is like. Now gently allow your sensing to flow from the Heart and from your head at the same time. What is that like? Do they complement each other? Now include the belly. Don't worry if you are doing it right. Just allow awareness to flow from all three places to whatever degree it is doing that. What is that like? How is it to have so many channels of information and awareness simultaneously? What is it like to sense, listen, and look from all three? Pick an object and sense it from all three places. How is that?*

What you really are is pure awareness—empty space that has this miraculous ability to sense the world. While this space is shaped by life and the human containers it passes through, its fundamental nature as space is not changed. By allowing it to flow through your true Heart (including your head, chest, and belly), you give it the most room to expand and function. Life is a rich and ever-changing challenge, so why not meet it with everything you are? From here on, when it is suggested that you allow awareness to flow from your Heart, that is also an invitation to allow it to flow from all of your Being—from the head, the belly, and the Heart. Your true Heart encompasses all of these and more.

LOOKING FROM SPACE ITSELF

The aware space of your Being is limitless and infinite. As you move more fully into looking from the Heart, you are also moving into a fuller experience of this infinite Presence of your Being. It is possible to drop even farther into your Being and look or sense from there. Awareness is a quality of the space itself and not contained in your head, chest, or belly. What actually senses is this infinite space that is all around the physical body.

> **Exercise:** *Try this exercise first with your eyes closed and then open. Notice what you are aware of in this moment: the sounds, a thought, or the objects around you. Notice if you are looking, listening, or sensing from the head, and notice what that is like. Now gently*

allow your sensing to flow from the Heart, the belly, and the head all at once. What is that like? Now allow your perspective to drop more deeply into the infinite space of your Being. You can look from everywhere and nowhere in particular. Don't worry if you are doing it right. Just allow awareness to flow from the depths of Being itself to whatever degree it is flowing. What is that like? What is it like to have so much of your sensing open and flowing? Allow what you are seeing and sensing to be seen and sensed by the empty space of Being. What is it like to sense, listen, and look from vast spaciousness? Pick an object and sense it with the limitless space of Being. How is that?

Your awareness doesn't always need to orient to your body. It can move directly from the infinite Presence of your Being. When awareness moves in this way, it is unshaped by any imprinting or conditioning. You can profoundly rest as this Space while awareness moves freely in whatever way it is happening to flow.

Exercise: *Allow your awareness to flow from the limitless space in the depth of your Being. It doesn't really matter what you are aware of, just where you are aware from. Now just settle in. Allow yourself to rest* *here in the vastness of Being's perspective. From here, there is only space.*

CHAPTER 4

It Isn't Always Easy

THE HUMAN CONDITION OF IMPRINTING

Your existence in human form means that the imprinting, or conditioning, you have received has many dimensions. It is not as simple as the baby duck's imprinting. Everything you experience imprints, or conditions, you to some degree. Your awareness is just that sensitive to life. You have been imprinted by your DNA, parents, teachers, siblings, acquaintances, environment, astrology, past lives, and the media. Add to this, every experience you have had, and you have quite a symphony of influences affecting the unfolding of your life and your awareness. Fortunately, you are not to blame for any of your conditioning. No one is to blame, or you could say everyone is equally to blame, since we all share our conditioning with others whenever we interact with them.

The net result of all this conditioning is that it isn't always easy to shift your awareness and look from your Heart or from your belly. It's always simple, but not always easy. For example, if you grew up with very intellectual parents or if you have been rewarded for your mind's capacity throughout school and work, the tendency to look from the mind may be especially strong.

In addition, if negative associations were formed around the body or the emotional side of life, it may be difficult for you to move into the belly or the Heart. When you do, you may experience discomfort that blocks your ability to perceive from that place. For instance, instead of a sense of solidity or strength in your belly, you may experience the opposite—a lack of support and stability there. Or you may find that awareness seems to contract when you move into your Heart because of some unresolved pain or hurt that seems to reside in your chest.

When these experiences arise, it is not a sign of anything wrong with you or your awareness. It's just another layer of imprinting that has accumulated. You didn't do anything to put it there; you just inherited it. The invitation is to simply stay with your experience no matter what happens. Sometimes if you sink a little deeper and sense the lack, resistance, pain, or blankness from even deeper in your Heart or belly, this can allow you to finally see the truth of that pain or resistance.

From the more complete view of the Heart, it will at least seem less significant.

Other times, it is necessary to stay present to the experience you are having for as long as it continues to arise. These hurt, scared, or seeming places of lack are actually just in need of simple acceptance and love. Staying with them is often all you need to do.

It is also fine to get help with anything that is stirred up by these new modes of awareness. Sometimes, just the caring, listening presence of another person is enough to allow you to stay with your experience as it unfolds.

START WHERE YOU ARE

If you are interested in discovering the truth of your awareness and what its possibilities are, the best place to do it is where awareness exists, and awareness is always right where you are. After all, it is what you are, so where else could it be?

The key to all spiritual practices is to apply them to your actual experience as it is right now. An idea of how you need to be different or what needs to change is just another thought that filters and shapes your awareness. Meanwhile here you are.

Exercise: *Allow your awareness to flow from the Heart, head, and belly as fully as you can to the conditions of your existence right now—to whatever* *sensations are present, whatever thoughts are arising, whatever blocks or difficulties are being triggered, whatever is happening right now. Relax and simply be aware of what is happening right now—because that's all there is to be aware of. Allow yourself to rest from trying to change any of it or trying to stop it if it is changing. It doesn't matter what you are experiencing. What matters is where you are experiencing it from, and that is true even of the difficult or painful experiences.*

GIVING SPACE

When it seems especially difficult or even impossible to move into your Heart or belly and look from there, another way to move into a more spacious perspective is to simply give space to your experience. You can give space to your sensations, thoughts, feelings, and the physical objects and events occurring around you. You can give space to whatever is appearing in your experience right now.

You are unlimited, aware space, so you don't need to pick and choose what you are aware of and what you allow into your experience. You can just give it all space to be here. Imagine if you were a multi-trillionaire. Having essentially limitless money would mean you could give lots of it away and still not run out. You are like a multi-multi-trillionaire when it comes to spacious awareness. You truly can't run out. You can give space to anything that shows up.

When you give space to your experiences, it shifts you more fully into the spaciousness of your Being, which is experienced in the Heart. You can imagine space flowing to or around the objects and sensations, or you can simply notice that there is already space for them. A simple test to determine if there is space for something is to notice if it exists: If something exists, there must be enough space for it to exist.

> **Exercise:** *Experiment giving aspects of your experience space. Imagine space flowing to them or around them. Or simply notice that the objects and events around you and within you already do have enough space to exist. Give space to your body and sensations just as they are. Give space to your thoughts, feelings, and desires. Give space to the objects in the room. Give space to the sounds appearing in your environment. Give lots of space to everything you can notice right now. What is that like? How spacious and free do you feel when you give space to everything?*
>
> *There's no need to be stingy—give things as much space as they need and more. If some aspect of your experience seems difficult or uncomfortable, then give it lots and lots of space. What happens if you give that difficulty or discomfort all of the space in your*

neighborhood? How about if you give it as much space
as the entire country you are in? Or all of the space in
the world or the solar system? How important does it
seem now? What else do you notice about that difficulty
or discomfort when you are giving it lots of space?

It can be helpful to start experimenting with giving space to something neutral like a piece of furniture or the sounds of birds outside. Once you have a sense of your capacity to give space to your experiences, you can experiment with giving space to more challenging, difficult, or painful aspects of your life.

Don't worry too much about what it actually means to "give something space." Even if the experiment of giving space is mostly intellectual at first, it can still put you in touch with that space. And since that aware space is what you are, it also puts you more in contact with your true nature.

Much of the time we have a sense of being limited. It seems like there is only so much time and awareness available, so we feel the need to pick and choose what we give our awareness to. We try to withdraw awareness from events or circumstances we don't like or want and focus it on what we do want.

The key is to give space and awareness to everything. You can give space to *both* your thoughts *and* your sensations. You can give space to *both* an external event *and* the feelings it evokes within you. You can give space to *both* a sense of excitement *and* a sense of fear about the same event *and* any doubts or worries you have about it *and* any memories that get triggered *and* any insights that arise in the midst of all these other responses. You can always give space to this and that and everything else.

> **Exercise:** *Notice something that is happening in your environment or, more generally, in your life right now. As you give space to this, also give space to the thoughts appearing in your mind about it. Simultaneously, give space to the feelings or desires you have about it. Give as much space as all of these events and internal reactions need and more. You can't run out of space. As you continue to give space to these things, also give space to everything else in your environment: other people, unrelated events and objects, and unrelated thoughts and feelings. Notice that you can just keep giving space to more and more of what makes up your life and experience. What is that like? Are you only in your head right now, or are you experiencing more fully from your whole Being, including your Heart and belly?*

Much of the time you can simply drop down and look from the Heart and/or belly, and the flow of spacious awareness will open up naturally. However, when you can't seem to stop thinking and looking from your head, then to loosen things up, give that experience some space. Then see if you can drop more easily into your Heart and belly. Giving space is another way to contact this spacious awareness that you are. As you give more space to your experience, awareness naturally shifts into the Heart and belly.

WHEN TO STOP

The point of these exercises is to bring you more in touch with your essential nature as aware space. Once you experience the potential of transforming your experience by looking from the Heart, you can simply rest and allow awareness to move in whatever way it most naturally wants to move. You are still aware space no matter where it is flowing from or how it is being shaped by your head, Heart, or belly.

How do you know when these exercises have served their purpose and it's time to rest and allow awareness its free and natural expression? The simple indicator is if, in the absence of any particular demand on awareness, your awareness naturally drops into the Heart and beyond, into the depths of Being itself. Because there is so much momentum to looking from the head, it is important to practice the alternatives. But once the new habits of looking from the Heart and belly or of giving things space are well established and you are doing this as often or more often than looking from the head, then there is no need for further practice. How long this takes will vary.

Life is full of challenges, opportunities, and profound mysteries. Why not bring all of your Being's capacities to this incredible journey called life? But remember, the ultimate goal is simply to rest in the Heart. It is your true home.

CHAPTER 5

The Heart in Everyday Life

CLEAR THINKING

We are strongly conditioned to watch our thoughts. The sheer volume of thoughts can be overwhelming. We think and think and then think some more. Often our thoughts are contradictory or irrelevant. How do you make sense of all this mental activity? How do you distinguish what is important and what is just idle chatter?

The important thing is to get some distance from your thoughts. Just as a painter needs to step back from the painting to get perspective on what he or she is doing, you need to step back from your mind and get some perspective. The simplest way to do this is to drop down into your Heart and belly and view your thoughts from there.

Exercise: *First, simply observe your thoughts. Notice the overall quality of your thinking. How much are you thinking right now? Are you quietly observing this moment's events? Or is there an endless stream of commentary and judgment or, perhaps, fantasizing about what should or shouldn't happen? Now allow yourself to drop down and experience your thoughts from the fullness of your Being in your Heart and belly. Without changing the nature or quantity of thoughts, what is your perspective on your thoughts when you experience them from down here? Can you sense the overall patterns of your thoughts more easily? Do they seem as important or meaningful? Can you more easily distinguish which thoughts are important or meaningful? Whenever you find yourself lost in thought or analysis, you can drop down into the Heart and regain perspective.*

There's nothing wrong with thought. It is sometimes useful and often entertaining. What matters is where you are experiencing your thoughts from. When you look at them from your head and focus narrowly on them, they seem much more relevant and important than they really are. In reality, most thoughts are irrelevant. For instance, the thought "What if I get a flat tire and am late to my appointment?" isn't relevant unless you actually get a flat tire, and even then, it doesn't contribute anything. And yet, our minds generate thousands of irrelevant thoughts each day. Nevertheless, every now and then a thought pops into the mind that is useful and relevant. For instance, you may have the thought "Remember to pick up the dry cleaning," and it is actually time to pick up the dry cleaning. The important thing is to be able to discriminate between relevant and irrelevant thoughts.

When you experience thoughts from the head, the focused quality of your awareness magnifies the content of the thought. Your thoughts seem very big or loud and therefore very important. In contrast, when you drop down and experience the mind's images or words from the depth of Being, they become actual size—which is very small. From here, there is no need to get rid of thoughts or even go to battle with them. If one of them happens to be relevant, it will still be noticed and acted on.

Find out what it's like to experience your thoughts from the deepest places in your Being. Find out what it's like to have some distance and perspective on the contents of your own mind. The open, spacious awareness that you are is also very wise and discriminating. Given a wide enough view, it can easily determine what is important and what isn't so important in the moment.

EMOTIONS

Feelings are like thoughts on steroids. If your usual experience of thought is like having your nose pressed against a TV screen, a strong feeling can be more like being at an IMAX theatre with a 10,000 watt sound system. While the energetic impression of a strong emotion can arise in your chest, belly, or throat, what matters is where you are experiencing the feeling from. If you stay in your head as a strong emotion arises, the emotion is often experienced as an internal conflict or split. You are in the head, and the feelings are down in the body, and it can be quite a challenge to manage them from up in the head. Because an emotion may seem huge and overwhelming, you may resist or deny it.

When you suppress or deny your feelings, it works for a while. But since the feelings haven't really gone away, they eventually resurface. At that point, the expression of the feeling is often like an explosion of pent up energy. When you finally are able to cry or yell or throw things, you feel a profound sense of release. However, all of this expression often creates a mess. The sense of relief from releasing these feelings is often followed by regret or guilt over what we said or did.

The mind is not a very good manager of the energy of emotions. It tends to magnify feelings and the thoughts generated by them. This magnification is what makes it seem important to suppress the feelings or release them through expression.

Another possibility is to drop into the Heart and experience the feeling from an open, spacious perspective. From the infinite space of Being, even a very strong emotion is not that significant. When there is so much space available for feelings, then suppressing or expressing them is not as necessary.

> **Exercise:** *Remember a recent experience that triggered a strong emotion in you. As much as possible, allow yourself to feel the feelings you had. Then drop into the depth of your Heart and especially your belly, if it is difficult to contain or stay with the feelings. Remember that you can also simply give space to the feeling, as much space as it needs. How important is the feeling when you give it lots of space and experience it from deep within? Is there room for the feeling to be here just the way it is? As you rest ever more deeply in the Heart and belly, do you really need to suppress your feelings or vent them?*

When you explore your feelings this way, be gentle and patient with yourself. Feelings often have strong charges and sensations associated with them that can be very difficult to experience. It may be helpful to find a therapist, counselor, spiritual guide, or group that is supportive of this kind of exploration.

As you practice dropping into the Heart and belly, or simply giving space to your strong emotions, you will find that it becomes much easier to experience, explore, and understand your feelings. Much of the energy and charged quality of your emotions is on the surface of your feelings, so when you look at your feelings from the outside with your mind, they can seem painful or overwhelming. However, when you drop into the Heart, those same feelings can be experienced as rich and full, without the sense of pressure or overwhelm. From the spacious, openness of true Being, there is plenty of room for strong emotions to arise.

When a strong emotion is present, you may find it difficult to drop into your Heart. This is because, as you drop into your Heart, you are starting to move inside the emotion rather than remain on the surface of it. Since most of the energy and sensations associated with your feelings are on the surface of them, as you drop into your Heart, you also drop through the energetically charged surface. This can be like jumping through a hoop of fire: It's only hot if you stop halfway through. With experience, you will find that it gets easier to trust dropping into the Heart when a strong emotion is triggered. While it may be more intense at first, the end result is a profound softening and relaxation of the struggle to contain or express your feelings.

What if you have within you the space and limitless capacity to really feel your most intense emotions? What if there is no problem with feelings as long as there is enough space for them to be here? What if you could just allow them to be here without having to exert yourself to suppress or resist them? What if you could allow them to be here so completely that you didn't even need to express or release them?

You may be surprised to find that it is possible to enjoy the richness and fullness of emotional energies when there is so much room, or space, for them in your Heart and Being. When something like anger or sadness arises, you may even find it is more satisfying to just feel it rather than express it. Why waste all that red hot energy of anger on somebody else? Why not just let it warm you and fill you with strength? With a big enough container, all of your emotions can add to the fullness of life. In your true Being, you already have a big enough container.

DESIRE

Desires push and pull us in so many directions. It is as if we are magnetized to what we desire: When you see or even think about something you want, you are irresistibly drawn to move toward it. On top of this, you have lots of contradictory desires, which leave you with internal conflicts: "I want to eat more, and I want to lose weight." "I want a relationship, and I want to be independent." "I want to buy a vacation house, and I want to simplify my life." However, desire is also normal and natural. It's what fuels many of our actions and accomplishments.

What really matters is not what desires you have, but where you experience them from. When you experience a desire from the head, you are on the surface of it and feeling the full force of wanting, as it draws you toward the object of your desire. When you drop into the Heart and experience the same desire from deeper within, you are taken to the source of the desire, where the force of the magnetic pull is less powerful. The desire is still present, but you are resting in the quiet source of your impulse to act.

The difference is like being in the rushing water of a giant spillway versus resting in the lake that is the source of the spillway. If you stay in your head, with its magnified focus on the object of desire, that is like being in the rushing water that is destined to flow over the spillway. From there, it's extremely difficult to resist the flow of desire, and most of the time, we don't. However, when you drop into your Heart and belly, it's like being in the center of the lake, where the water is still and calm. The spillway of your desire is still present, but there is more choice about whether or not to act on it.

Exercise: *Think of something you really want—a possession or an experience you desire. As you think about it, notice what that is like. Can you feel the* *magnetic pull of that object of desire? As you continue to focus on it with your mind, it may seem more and more important and irresistible. Now move down into the Heart and/or belly and experience your desire from there. You don't need to change your desire. Just experience the same pull from deep within your Being. How important is the desire when you feel it from the Heart and belly? Is it easier to resist the pull, to just rest in the spaciousness of your Being?*

As you rest deeply in your Heart, it is more possible to see the full range of your desires and impulses. You have many desires. Since you do have so many, including contradictory and unhealthy ones, it can be helpful to rest in the Heart, where you can more easily see which ones are true and valuable. Even very strong contradictory desires are not a problem when you are resting in the center of your Being, where they don't have so much leverage.

Exercise: *Take a moment to list several of the desires you have in this moment. Be sure to include any contradictory or opposite ones, which create internal conflicts (e.g., wanting to eat more and wanting to lose weight). Notice what it's like to have all these desires. Do you feel pulled this way and that by them? Can you feel how some desires pull you in opposite directions?*

Now drop into your Heart and/or belly and consider the full range of your desires from deep within. Here in the stillness of your Being, how important are your desires? When you rest in the center of your Being, do they push and pull you as strongly? Take a moment to consider from your Heart which desires are worth acting on and which are not.

When you experience desires with the mind, trying to manage all the impulses you have around them can be exhausting. Even when you satisfy one, it usually stirs up an opposite one. This is why we end up in yo-yo patterns of behavior. In contrast, when you experience desires from your Heart and belly, satisfying them is not so important. Paradoxically, this makes it easier to see how to respond to them.

This practice of experiencing desires from the Heart and belly can be especially useful in regard to addictions or compulsions. Addictions are desires we have been so strongly imprinted or conditioned to pay attention to that they often seem truly irresistible. Nevertheless, if you rest more deeply in your Being, it is possible to resist them. With any very strong impulse or addiction, it is especially helpful to move all the way down into the belly and experience the desire from there. The belly is a place of solidity and grounding. Dropping all the way into your belly is like sinking to the bottom of the lake and becoming a giant boulder. Even the strongest spillways of desperate desire won't be able to move you from the mountain of Presence in your belly.

The Buddha said that desire is the cause of all suffering. And yet, the end of your suffering isn't dependent on getting rid of your desires, but on simply moving into the depths of your Being and experiencing them from a place where they have much less pull. Your suffering is the internal conflict you experience when you are so mentally involved with your desires that you feel you must satisfy or resist them. As you move into the Heart and belly, your desires no longer push and pull on you so strongly, and the effort to control them or satisfy them is no longer there, and neither is the suffering. Being in the Heart allows you to be at peace internally while you move through life.

RELATIONSHIPS

Your life is full of relationships: with people, objects, nature, the world, and society in general. Your experience of these relationships is affected by your conditioning. The good news is you don't have to get rid of the conditioning that limits or diminishes your ability to be fulfilled in your relationships. When this conditioning arises in relationships, you can simply allow your awareness to flow from the Heart and belly rather than from the mind.

Exercise: *Think of someone in your life you are having difficulty with. For a moment, allow yourself to experience all the reactions and judgments this person evokes. Notice what it's like to be very involved with thoughts about this person. Allow any thoughts that arise, and notice what it's like to experience them from the head. Really focus on the details of your relationship: what he or she said or did, how he or she said or did it, etc. Now drop into your Heart and/or belly as you continue to consider that person. What is it like to experience someone from the Heart and belly? You don't have to change anything about what he or she did or said. Give that person space to be the way he or she is, and give yourself space to feel the way you feel. Notice what the experience of that person is like from your Heart. Is there more ability to allow that person to be the way he or she is? Are you able to perceive more of his or her true nature?*

Sometimes we are afraid that if we don't defend ourselves with judgments, we will be a doormat to the undesirable behaviors of others. However, when we are busy with our thoughts and judgments, we aren't able to be present to others in the moment. Our thoughts and judgments keep us at a distance from reality and interfere with relating to others as they are in the moment. As you experience others from the

Heart and belly, all of your senses and observations are flowing freely, and you can respond to what is actually present or happening. When your awareness flows from the belly, you are especially able to act or respond appropriately with strength and firmness if that is needed.

> **Exercise:** *Imagine or remember a situation where someone confronts you with criticism or conflict. Notice what it is like as you think about the situation from your head. Now drop your awareness into your belly. Take a moment to really experience the firmness or strength that flows from here. What is it like to consider the criticism or conflict from this place of solid Presence? How important or overwhelming does the criticism or conflict seem when you are experiencing it from a spacious and solid center? Try dropping into your belly just before and during any challenging interactions that come up in your life.*

We have been conditioned to pay lots of attention to others, either to protect ourselves or to be nice and take care of others. Unfortunately, because our attention or awareness seems limited, we often abandon ourselves to take care of others. It can be a big relief to discover that there is enough awareness available to pay attention to others and also stay in full contact with our own experience and Being.

Exercise: *Imagine or remember a situation where you were very focused on someone else and his or her needs. Notice what it is like to focus (from your mind) on what is happening for that person and what he or she wants. Where are you when your focus is totally on that person? Now drop into your Heart and/or belly and allow awareness to flow equally and freely to the other person and to your own sensations and responses. See if you can fully sense that person's presence and needs and, at the same time, fully sense your own presence and needs. The openness of awareness that flows from your Heart and belly is available for everyone present—including you!*

In addition to being the source of many challenges, relationships are also the source of great joy and satisfaction. Why not experience the richness of life's gifts from a place of openness and full awareness?

Exercise: *Think of someone you feel great love or appreciation for. For a moment, just think about that person only from your head. Notice the degree of connectedness and intimacy you can experience through the head. Now drop down into the fullness of your Heart and belly and allow your love and appreciation to flow from the depths of your Being. How is it to experience this fuller flow of connection* *and intimacy? Try dropping into your Heart and belly just before and during any intimate and joyful interaction that comes up in your life.*

Surprisingly, we can also abandon ourselves when we focus positively on others. We project all of the goodness and joy onto them, and we may even become overly attached because we assume they are the source of that joy and fulfillment. Even in the most satisfying moments of deep contact and enjoyment with others, there is enough awareness available to include your own Being and the limitless source of joy that you are.

Exercise: *Imagine or remember a moment when you found great joy in another. Notice what it's like to focus entirely on that person with your Heart as you experience his or her goodness and presence. Now drop deeply into your Heart and belly and notice what it's like to also be fully aware of the goodness and presence in your own Being. There is goodness and presence in everyone—including you!*

THE BODY

We are strongly imprinted onto and identified with our physical bodies, so much so that it can seem crazy to even question the belief "I am the body." Underlying this belief is the belief that the physical dimension of life is the most real. We believe in something when we can see, hear, or touch it. While there is nothing wrong with or bad about the physical world or our bodies, such a strong focus on that dimension of life is limiting. We can be so involved with the experiences on the physical level that we overlook, discount, or deny the experiences of more subtle dimensions.

Over-involvement and identification with the body can also cause a lot of suffering. How we look or feel physically can seem too important, and we suffer over it. The suffering doesn't actually come from our physical reality, but from any judgments and excessive effort to change, improve, or protect the body. Our true nature is much more vast and spacious than our physical form and appearance, but when we struggle to change or improve the physical, we suffer.

Doing things to take care of the body, like eating well and exercising, is not a problem of course. The problem is an over-involvement with our body image and judgments about our body. We can be so involved with our images, fears, doubts, and worries about our bodies that we don't experience the body as it is. The body-image can seem more real than the body itself. This image is often felt to be inferior and require a lot to make it better.

Fortunately, the antidote to this suffering is not to improve your body image, but to experience your ideas about the body and the body itself from deeper within your Being. Without changing what you think or what you look like, you can experience all of that from your Heart. The body and your judgments of it become much less important when seen from the Heart. You can sense the spaciousness of Being in which the body and your body-images appear. What you are is that space, and the body is only a small part of what appears within you. There is also your love, wisdom, compassion, strength and the simple miracle of your awareness. These non-physical dimensions of your Being are actually much larger and more real than the body.

This broader perspective doesn't disconnect you from your body or physical sensations, even if they no longer seem so important. Instead, putting physical reality into perspective frees you to fully experience the richness of experience available in the physical world. When it's not so important to change or improve your body and sensory experiences, you can simply enjoy your body as it is.

Exercise: *Take a moment to notice your body. Observe how you are currently experiencing the body and notice the thoughts, feelings, and desires that arise when you consider your body. Now notice where you are experiencing your body from. If you are experiencing it from your head, notice what that is like. Do you really feel your body from up in your head, or are you mostly thinking about it? Notice any judgments, fears, worries,* *pride, resentments, or attachments you have in regard to your body.*

Now drop down into your Heart and belly and experience the body from deep within your Being. Continue to notice all the ideas, beliefs, and reactions you have to the body that are going on in your head. Then sense the physical form of your arms, legs, and torso from deep within. What are the physical sensations of your body like when you experience them from your Heart and belly? How important are they?

Can you sense the open, spacious awareness that your body and so much more of your Being is appearing in? Can you sense the field of awareness the body appears in and the many other rich dimensions to your Being in that open awareness? Check if there is any peace, love, compassion, or curiosity in your awareness. How important is it to fix or change your body when you experience it from deep within? How important is your body when you can also sense many other dimensions of your Being?

While you rest more deeply in the spaciousness of your Heart, remember to also give space to the body. Give it the space to be the way it is in this moment. Return to the physical sensations of your body in this moment and experience them from the Heart with this expanded perspective. Notice if there are sensations of heat or coolness. Notice any pressure or texture to the objects you are touching. Notice any sounds, visual sensations, or internal sensations of the body as you breathe and digest your most recent meal. Does resting in the Heart allow you to experience the physical sensations of your body more fully?

The body is one of the more miraculous creations of your Being. Shifting out of the head, where over-identification with the body occurs, allows you to more completely experience the incredible symphony of physical sensation going on in every moment without the suffering caused by endlessly trying to fix or change your body. There is enough space and awareness for every amazing bodily experience that life offers and also for all of the other dimensions of your Being. Dropping into the Heart allows the richness of life to be met and enjoyed.

PAIN

Enjoying the body sounds great, but what about when you are in pain? Physical pain is there for a reason. It's usually telling us that something in the body is out of balance or needs attention. The pain of a blister is there so that you will stop and put on a band-aid. The continuing pain of a physical illness or injury is there so that you will get treatment or rest. A life without the capacity to feel pain would be dangerous and disastrous. So it's important to recognize the message in pain and respond to it.

Having said that, it's possible to have pain but not suffer over it. Suffering doesn't come from physical pain, but from our judgments about it, our resistance to it, and our struggle to change it. When we experience pain through the head, the experience is strongly colored by all our beliefs and fears about pain and what it may mean in terms of our safety, future, and wellbeing. Because of what we believe about it, pain scares us, so we struggle against it. Our suffering actually comes from these beliefs and fears and our struggle to get away from the pain—not from the pain itself, which is only sensations. We learn to associate the sensations of pain with the internal experience of suffering and struggle.

This association of pain with suffering and struggle can make the pain worse. In his books about back pain and mind-body medicine, Dr. John Sarno explains how anxiety about pain triggers physiological responses that cause more pain. This can become a vicious cycle, in which our beliefs about pain cause more pain, which triggers more fear and then more pain.

One way to interrupt this cycle is to give space to the physical sensations just as they are and then drop into the Heart, where it is easier to experience the sensations directly. From the Heart, it's possible to separate the experience of physical sensations from thoughts and beliefs about them and thereby eliminate suffering.

Exercise: *Notice if there are any painful sensations in your body right now. It's best to start with something simple, like a minor ache or even just an itch. If there are no painful sensations present, then remember a physical pain you had in the past and work with that. Repeat this exercise when you are having some pain.*

Notice all of your thoughts, feelings, and reactions to the painful sensation. See if you can discover some of the beliefs, especially the fears you have regarding pain.

Notice where you are experiencing the pain and the thoughts from. If you are experiencing them through the head, what is that like? How important does the pain seem? How important do any fears, doubts, or worries about the pain seem when you experience them through your head?

Now drop down into your Heart or your belly and experience the sensations and thoughts from there. What is that like? How important is the painful sensation from this grounded and spacious perspective? How important are any fears, doubts, or worries that are happening in the head? Take some time to sense the physical sensations you are experiencing while resting deeply in your Being. What is the sensation itself like if you pay full attention to it and, for a moment, just give space to the thoughts and fears in the head without paying attention to them? What are the pure sensations like? Is there one constant sensation or an ever-changing series of sensations in the painful area? Exactly where is the sensation located? What is the quality of the sensation right now, and what is it like in the next moment? Give space to the sensations as they occur and rest as deeply as possible in the Heart or belly.

As you continue to give your full attention to the sensations in your body moment to moment, notice what the overall quality of your experience is like. Are you able to relax with the pain when you give it your full attention, as you rest more deeply in your Heart? Is there as much of a sense that the pain is a problem, or is the pain more of an experience of ever-changing sensations? Do the sensations have the quality of suffering when you experience them this way? Or are they more bearable, or at least less uncomfortable, when you experience them from your Heart? Is it possible that the suffering comes from the magnified experience of judgment and fear that happens when you are in your head and caught up in your thoughts about the pain? Is there less or possibly even no discomfort in the sensations when you experience them free of the coloring of your mind's comments and projected fears?

Especially if there is some kind of chronic painful condition, take some time to rest deeply in this more relaxed open place of simple sensation. Give yourself a moment's rest from the struggle to fix or change the sensations.

You can still do whatever is indicated to take care of your body and any painful messages it is sending you. As you take action to relieve or correct a painful condition, continue to explore the truth of where the suffering comes from. Is it possible to experience pain from a depth of your Being where there is no resistance to the situation and therefore no real suffering over it?

It is best to begin this exploration with something simple, like a minor ache or other relatively small pain, before you attempt to discern the true source of suffering in a strong pain. However, it is profound to discover that the same principle applies to the more painful conditions that can arise. Imagine how freeing it would be to discover that even extreme pain is not the cause of your suffering—that you can always drop into the spaciousness of Being and experience the most difficult sensations from there. While you still need to do whatever is within your power to correct or relieve the pain, the perspective of the Heart offers a simple way to reduce or relieve the suffering that is so often associated with physical pain.

DEATH AND LOSS

In some spiritual traditions, life—and particularly the experience of loss—is seen as an opportunity to practice for the ultimate loss: death. The belief is that if you can remain fully present and aware at the actual moment of physical death, it is a sign that you are free of the limited perspectives that cause all suffering. Everything short of death, when the stakes are not as high, is an opportunity to explore this possibility. You have all the rich and varied experiences of ordinary life to practice with before you meet the moment of your death.

Just as physical pain is one of the more challenging experiences to meet with an open Heart and a full and grounded perspective, so are the moments when we are confronted with death or loss. Like pain, death and loss stir up all our fears. These moments are opportunities to explore the truth of your mortality and the impermanence of everything and everybody you love. Why not explore this most challenging aspect of life from the wisest and most complete dimension of your Being? Why not face death, your own or others, from your Heart instead of just with your mind?

Exercise: *Take a moment to sense the possibility of your own death. You can also do this exercise by sensing the possibility of the death or loss of anything or anyone you hold dear. Allow yourself to consider the many consequences of the end of your physical existence or the loss of someone or something. Notice all the thoughts, feelings, desires, reactions, fears, and beliefs that are stirred up by considering this. Now notice where you are experiencing these thoughts and feelings from. If you are mostly experiencing them through your head, what is that like? How important or difficult does death or loss seem to be from that perspective?*

Now drop deeply into your Heart and allow the awareness of the same possibility of death or loss to flow from the most open, spacious dimensions of your Being. How is it to sense this possibility from your depths? How important or difficult does death or loss seem from deep within awareness itself? Take some time to rest here in the Heart and sense the endless flow of time through all comings and goings of form and experience. Drop as deeply as you can into the spacious awareness in which your body appears and into which it will return.

You can return to this exploration again whenever the thought of death or loss arises, especially if you or someone you care about is facing this possibility. While it is inherently freeing and liberating to discover that your true nature is limitless eternal space, this discovery is especially profound if you are facing a death or loss. Space itself cannot be harmed or diminished in any way. What a profound gift to recognize that space is what you actually are and what you always will be.

CHAPTER 6

What Is Going on Here?

THE QUALITIES OF AWARENESS

The exercises and practices offered here can profoundly shift the way you experience your life, the events, and the people in it. When you experience your everyday life from your Heart, it can seem like you are living in a completely new world. And in a sense, that is true. It is a world where what happens is less important than where you are experiencing it from.

Why does this shift to looking from the Heart have such a profound effect on your experience? Even when it doesn't actually change what is happening, the difference can be transformative. This is because looking from the Heart shifts you more fully into your own Being, your true nature. While you are made of aware space, it is not exactly empty space. Everything that really matters is found in the space that you are, not in the external events or experiences of life, as we so often assume. For example, the experience of joy or happiness is a natural quality of the openness of aware space. When your awareness opens up and flows more freely, you naturally become more joyful and fulfilled. This happiness is inherent to Being, so life naturally becomes a fuller and richer experience as you move more fully into the space of your Being.

This can and does also happen when external circumstances line up with your desires. However, this is only because the desire has been fulfilled, so your awareness relaxes and expands, and in that expanded awareness is an experience of joy and happiness—for the moment. Unfortunately, we often mistakenly assume that the external circumstance is the source of the happiness, when the true source is actually the spaciousness of your Being.

The same principle applies to everything that really matters in life: love, peace, worthiness or value, compassion, clarity, wisdom, strength, beauty, and perfection. These very real and important experiences are qualities of the space that you are. So anything that opens up your experience of this spaciousness can put you more in touch with these qualities of Being. Anytime you have been in contact with the truly meaningful dimensions of life, you have been contacting this spacious awareness of your Being and the qualities inherent in it.

IT IS ALL DIVINE NATURE

The experience of looking from the Heart is quite different from looking from the head, but the looking itself is fundamentally the same. To contact your Being, it isn't necessary to look from the Heart or from anywhere in particular. While it's much easier to contact the nature of your Being when you look from the Heart, even when it is flowing less fully, it is still your true nature. The point of these exercises is to show you the nature of your Being so thoroughly that you can rest as that aware space.

Experiencing more fully the limitless nature of your Being is freeing. Discovering that this is always the nature of your Being, no matter what is shaping or limiting your experience of it, is even more freeing. You can rest in this essential awareness no matter what is happening or how you are experiencing it. Just as you don't need to see your car to know it exists, you don't need to have a rich and full experience of your Being in every moment to know it exists. It is always here. It's what is living you.

This alive awareness and spaciousness is the nature of you. It is your divine nature. You are divine. Even when you are contracted and confused, you are divine. It's all divine. That is all there is, and you are that.

WHAT ARE YOU?

It doesn't matter that much what you are experiencing in life. What matters is what you really *are*. Is it possible that you really are not the body, your personality, or your mind? Is it possible that these are things you experience but they are not what you are made of? Is it possible that you are space—an open and allowing space—that the body and mind appear in? What if this space is aware? What if it is really the space that is perceiving these words?

This space that you are is limitless. This space of Being has no boundaries. If you go on and on forever, what would that mean? What would it mean if there is unlimited awareness available in every moment? Would you still need to be so careful about what you experience and what you avoid? Or could you just allow every experience to have some of the limitless space that you are?

What if there is only one space? You are it, and so is everyone and everything. What if you already contain everything you could ever desire or want to experience? What if you already are everything you want to become?

What if this space is alive? What if space itself is the aliveness you feel right now? What if this space is full of peace, joy, and love? What if this space is already full and rich and satisfying in ways that the experiences of the world have never been? What if this space is you?

Exercise: *Take a moment to reread the last five paragraphs while resting deeply in your Heart. Take each question one at a time and hold it in awareness as you drop more deeply into the spaciousness of your Being. Don't worry about getting an answer or holding on to any answers that arise. The questions themselves will show you more and more of the truth of your nature.*

Like any good adventure, this exploration of your nature can bring you back to where you started, only with a transformed and more complete view. Where you start and where you end up is always in what you really are: aware space. Welcome home.

> *it is here*
> *in the breath*
> *it is here*
> *in the stillness between breaths*
>
> *it is here*
> *in the active mind*
> *it is here*
> *in the resting mind*

it is here
in the dream's panorama
it is here
in each moment of awakening

it is here
when all is well
it is here
when fear has nothing left to fear

even then
there is pure noticing
even then
there is no need for doing

no frantic searching
can find the obvious
no seeking needed
to find that which seeks

it is here
where it can never be lost or found

PART 2

The Heart's Wisdom

The Heart's Wisdom

The truth is that which opens the Heart. The capacity to sense the truth is something we all already have. We all have a Heart that is already accurately showing us how true things are.

Anything that puts you in touch with more of the truth opens the Heart. This is a literal and experiential description of truth. When your experience is bringing you more truth, there is a sense of opening, softening, relaxation, expansion, fulfillment, and satisfaction in the Heart. This can be most directly sensed in the center of the chest, but the Heart of all Being is infinite and therefore actually bigger than your entire body. So this opening, softening, and expansion is actually happening everywhere; we just sense it most clearly and directly in the center of the chest.

When you encounter truth, the sense of your self opens, expands, softens, fills in, and lets go. The *me,* the sense of your self, is no longer felt to be so limited or small. It becomes more complete and unbounded. The boundaries soften and dissolve, and any sense of inadequacy, limitation, or deficiency is lessened or eliminated.

As a side effect of being in touch with more of the truth, your mind gets quieter because you simply have less to think about. Even knowing a simple truth like where your car keys are gives you less to think about. And when you touch upon a very large truth, your mind becomes even quieter, like when you see the ocean for the first time: The truth or reality you're viewing is so immense that, at least for a moment, your mind is stopped and becomes very quiet.

In contrast, when your experience is moving into a diminished or smaller experience of the truth and of reality, the Heart contracts. The sense of your self gets tight, hard, contracted, and feels incomplete, bounded, and limited. It can feel like you are small, inadequate, or unworthy. The smallness of the truth is reflected in the smallness of the sense of your self. The result of being less in touch with the truth is that your mind gets busier as it tries to figure out what is true.

Fortunately, your Being is never diminished or contracted, only the *sense* of your self. Just as blocking your view of the whole room by partially covering your eyes makes your sense of the room smaller without actually making the room smaller, an idea or belief that is not very true is reflected in a small sense of your self, without actually limiting or contracting your Being.

This opening and closing of the Heart in response to the degree of truth you are experiencing isn't something you need to practice or perfect. Your Heart has been accurately and perfectly showing you how true your experience has been all along. If you start to notice your Heart's openings and closings, you'll discover that you already have everything you need to determine what is true. The Heart is the true inner teacher, the source of inner guidance we all have as our birthright. You don't need a spiritual teacher or spiritual books to show you what is true, just your own Heart.

Exercise: Take a moment to sense your Heart. Dropping into the Heart can help you get more in touch with what is happening there. Notice if the Heart feels relatively contracted or relatively open. In either case, your Heart is working perfectly to show you the degree of truth you are experiencing in this moment. Also notice if your Heart is expanding or contracting in this moment. The movement might be subtle or a fairly gross contraction or relaxation. You may be able to notice that the Heart is always shifting in response to every thought, feeling, desire, and experience that arises in your awareness. There is no wrong way for your Heart to respond. It is always showing you the relative truth of this moment.

WHAT IS THE TRUTH?

Truth is what exists, what is here now. So if what exists is also what is true, then there is only truth. Whatever is present is true—but to varying degrees. Just as there is no actual substance or energy that is darkness, but just varying amounts of the energy of light or photons, there is no falsehood or untruth, only varying degrees of the truth.

We are always experiencing the truth. But because we don't experience everything in any one moment, our experience of truth is always limited. Sometimes we experience a large amount of truth—of what is actually here—and sometimes we experience only a small amount of what is actually happening, of what is true. Our Heart's openness or lack of openness in each moment is what shows us how much of the truth is being experienced in any moment.

What about ideas that are mistaken? An idea or belief that has little or no correspondence to external reality is going to be an extremely small truth, so small it may only exist in one person's mind, like the saying: "He was a legend in his own mind." When you experience an erroneous idea or belief, your Heart will contract appropriately to show you that it is a very small and inconsequential truth.

For example, if you entertain the idea that you will never be happy unless you have ten million dollars, your Heart will contract appropriately to show you that it is just an idea. This contraction may be very quick, so quick that it doesn't cause you any discomfort or trouble. But if you really believe this, then the sense of your self will contract for as long as that idea is held.

Exercise: For just a moment, hold onto a limiting thought, such as "I will never have enough time," and notice the response in your Heart. Does that thought allow you to relax and be, or does it require a kind of effort or contraction just to hold it? Now consider another thought that you find ridiculous because it is so untrue, such as "I will never be happy unless I become President of the United States." Notice how it might not even be possible to hold onto this thought. It might even make you laugh. Many jokes end with a ridiculously impossible truth (e.g., "And then the dog said to its owner, 'I guess I should have said Dimaggio instead of Ruth') and the smallness of the truth of the punch line causes you to let go of believing in it. Laughter is a wonderful movement into a bigger perspective!

Thoughts are real—they exist—but they still exist only as ideas. You could put all the thoughts ever thought into a pile, and they still wouldn't trip anybody. They only exist as neural firings in the brain, so to focus on thoughts exclusively is to severely limit or contract your experience of reality and therefore the sense of your self.

In the range of everyday experience, our ideas have varying degrees of correspondence with reality. Those that correspond more closely to reality won't contract or limit the sense of self for as long as mistaken ones. Many ideas are of service to our ability to be at ease in the world. For example, when you need to go someplace, correct ideas about how to get there allow you to simply go there and then move on to other experiences. Ideas such as these can enhance our experience, rather than limit or contract it. An idea about where something is located is, of course, not a big truth, but it's also not usually experienced as a limiting one.

THE HEART'S CAPACITY TO SHOW YOU THE TRUTH

All there is, is truth, and our Heart's capacity to reflect the degree of truth in any experience is the way we recognize how true a particular experience is.

What is this Heart? What is this sense of self that is ever present? It doesn't relate to sensations in the physical heart or chest. It's a more subtle sense, at times even more subtle than the physical senses, although the opening or contracting can also be experienced as relaxation and contraction in the physical body. The sense of your self, the sense that you exist, is something more intimate than your physical experience.

What does it mean when you say *me*? What are you referring to when you say *me*? This simple fact that we are here, that we exist, is a very mysterious aspect of our experience. When we speak of it poetically to try to capture its essence, we call it the Heart, like when you know something in your Heart or when your Heart is touched.

This sense of your self is a very alive and changing experience. At times, your sense of *me* is open, free-flowing, and expanded. At other times, like when a judgment arises, it feels small, inadequate, and deficient. In these moments, have you actually changed? Has your body suddenly shrunk? Much of the time this sense of *me* is bigger than or smaller than your physical body. How does that work? Have you ever experienced your inner child? How can your *me* be the size of a child when you are an adult?

The sense of *me,* the sense of self, is shifting all the time. It's always either opening and expanding, or contracting and tightening, similar to the ongoing expansion and contraction of our breathing.

Exercise: Consider the idea that it is better to be thinner or more beautiful or younger than you are, and notice what happens to the sense of your self. Does your Heart open, soften, and expand? Does this idea allow you to simply be? Or does it tighten and restrict the flow of your experience?

Then just for contrast, notice what happens to the sense of your self if you consider the idea that you are okay just the way you are. It might be challenging to consider this idea without other thoughts being triggered, such as "But I'm not really good enough!" If this happens, your Heart will show you how true this response is, not how true the original idea of okayness is.

Just as an experiment, see if you can hold the idea that you're okay just the way you are, and then notice what happens in your Heart. Does this idea allow your Heart to open, soften, and expand? Does it allow you to simply be? Or does it tighten and restrict the flow of your experience? For most, the idea of being okay just the way they are allows a greater ease and fullness to the experience of the self.

The idea that it is better to be thinner, more beautiful, or younger than you are is simply a smaller truth than the idea that you are perfect the way you are. Even if you *are* beautiful, thin, or young, the idea that it is better to be that way can limit the sense of your self. If it's better to be that way, can you just relax and be, or do you need to do something to stay that way?

In contrast, a neutral idea that doesn't state or imply anything about you can be experienced neutrally in your sense of self. For example, if you consider the color of the ceiling in someone else's house, this usually won't open or close your

Heart because it's not about you and probably doesn't imply anything about you. The sense of your self doesn't shift in response to neutral ideas like this.

This opening and closing of the Heart is not a prescription—something you need to practice—but simply a description of what your Heart has been doing your entire life. Whatever does happen in the sense of self in any moment is entirely correct and appropriate. It's appropriate for your Heart to close when someone is telling you a small, limiting truth; and it's appropriate for your Heart to open when you experience a deep and profound reality.

THE HEART'S QUICKNESS

Your Heart is incredibly quick. It instantly knows how true something is and instantly opens or closes to that degree. It's so fast that it never really lands anywhere. It is always either opening or closing in response to each moment.

So if a thought triggers another thought, the Heart will then be reflecting the relative truth of the triggered thought, not the original one. And if this triggered thought triggers another one, then your Heart will reflect how true the latest thought is. The openness of your Heart can shift very rapidly, as rapidly as you can think another thought!

I was working with a woman once who had difficulty taking time for herself. I asked her to check in her Heart to see how true it is that it is okay to take time for herself. She closed her eyes for a moment, and when I asked her what had happened, she said she felt an intense contraction. I was surprised, so I asked her to tell me exactly what had happened. She said she thought, "It's okay to take time for myself," and then immediately decided this would be selfish, and her Heart contracted. Her Heart was showing her how true it was that it would be selfish to take time for herself. It was no longer reflecting the truth of the idea that it is okay to take time for herself.

In the quickness of our usual rapid-fire thinking, it can be tricky to determine what your Heart is actually responding to. Therefore, when checking in your Heart to see how true something is, it is helpful to slow down and take each thought or each possibility one at a time.

Exercise: Take a moment to think about a situation in your life. Notice if there are any familiar or recurring thoughts about that situation. Pick one of the main ideas, beliefs, opinions, or attitudes you have about that situation or about someone or something related to it. Now just hold that thought gently in your awareness. Repeat it to yourself a few times, and as you do, notice what happens in your Heart. Does it open and soften, or is there a kind of tightness or hardness that starts to form in your awareness?

Remember, either way your Heart is working perfectly to show you how true the thought is.

See if you can hold that one simple thought for a moment, almost like a child completely engrossed in whatever he or she is looking at. Holding a thought for a moment gives you a clearer picture of the relative truth of that thought, as indicated by your Heart's response while you are focusing completely on it.

If your mind wanders and you find yourself having second and third thoughts, or even a whole conversation with yourself about the situation, that's fine. Just note that the Heart has moved on along with your thoughts and is now showing you the truth of the thought you are having in this moment.

THE ROLE OF JUDGMENTS

Not only can an initial thought or experience trigger other thoughts, the opening or closing of your Heart can itself trigger a thought or judgment that results in the further closing of the Heart and a sense of your self as limited or small. If you are a spiritual seeker and have come to believe that it is better for your Heart to be open than closed, then a sudden contraction of the sense of your self can trigger a further judgment related to not wanting to be contracted, which closes the Heart even further. Test it for yourself:

Exercise: *If you hold the idea that you shouldn't feel contracted, does your Heart open? Does that idea allow you to just be? Or does it tighten or limit the sense of your self? The idea that you shouldn't feel contracted is a limiting idea and usually feels tight or limited because it is simply not very true.*

There is a certain kind of logic to this cycle of judgment, even though it results in a restricted sense of self: When the sense of your self contracts, your awareness also contracts and becomes limited, and your *un*awareness expands. When your field of awareness becomes smaller, the rest of reality lies outside your awareness in that moment. The logic of judgment is based on this simple effect. As a result of a judgment, you become less aware of your experience and temporarily less aware of the initial discomfort that triggered the judgment. Therefore, you get some relief from it. The logic of judgment is based on this temporary relief provided by the reduction in your awareness.

However, the flaw in this logic is that now that contraction of your awareness must be maintained or you will become aware again of the initial discomfort. Maintaining a contraction is, itself, uncomfortable. Try making a tight fist and holding it for several moments. It will quickly begin to feel uncomfortable. Similarly, when you keep your awareness contracted to avoid an uncomfortable sensation, this generates even more discomfort.

So when a cycle of judgment is triggered, the sense of your self and your awareness keep getting smaller as you try to avoid the ever-increasing discomfort caused by this same contraction of your sense of self and your awareness. This often continues until you are exhausted by the effort involved in maintaining vigilance against your discomfort, and you simply let go of any judgment.

The good news is that whenever you are not contracting your sense of self through small truths, such as judgments, the sense of your self naturally relaxes and opens. An open, spacious sense of self is the natural resting state of your Being, just as your muscles naturally lengthen and expand in the absence of any effort to contract them. So when a cycle of judgment wears you out, there is sometimes a profound release of the small sense of self and the contraction of awareness. In light of this, it's not surprising that many realizations and spiritual awakenings occur immediately following an extremely contracted and painful experience.

More good news is that the tendency to judge is not your fault. You were taught to do it by those who raised you, who were taught by those who raised them. They did this because it was the best way they knew to manage their own discomfort. When parents are confronted with the unlimited Being of a two year-old (and we all know how big that can be), they often resort to the best means they know for giving that two year-old a more limited sense of his or her Being: judgment.

We eventually learned to do this for ourselves. We learned to judge ourselves and hold limiting ideas about ourselves to get along with the people around us, especially those who clothed and fed us.

Judgment is just one of the many ways we limit our experience of the truth and thereby limit our experience of our self. Other culprits are our ideas, beliefs, opinions, concepts, doubts, fears, worries, hopes, dreams, desires, and our usual knowledge. Judgment is just one of the more effective ways of limiting the sense of our self because it always implies something limiting about the self.

Exercise: Make a list of some of the judgments you have about yourself, life, and other people. Pick ones that you really believe. Now read through your list several times and notice the sense you have of yourself as you do this. Does holding these judgments give you a sense of yourself as someone in particular, someone who has a very definite perspective on life? Do you feel more connected with others and with the world, or do you feel more separate and apart from the world? Even if that separate sense of self feels superior because it has the right judgments, how big or open and relaxed is your sense of self when you have these judgments?

This implied someone in all of your judgments is always a small someone, someone who is limited and therefore vulnerable to something bad or who needs to feel superior or for something good to happen to feel better or even survive. The ultimate truth is that you are unlimited. Your Being can never be harmed—or benefited—by any experience. Only a smaller (less true) idea of your self can seem to be harmed or benefited.

POSITIVE JUDGMENT

What was said about negative judgments applies to positive judgments as well. When some experience triggers a positive judgment, the sense of our self contracts just as much as when we have a negative judgment. Test this for yourself:

Exercise: Think about something you have a very strong positive judgment of, like your favorite movie or something you have done that you are very proud of. Notice what happens to the sense of your self when you have a positive thought about this. If you find yourself thinking something like, "Great! This is wonderful—wait until I tell my friends!" notice what happens to the sense of your self. You may be surprised to find that your Heart isn't as open as it was before the positive judgment. A big truth allows you to relax and just be however you are and to change in any way that naturally happens. A positive idea about your self implies that you have to continue to be a certain way to be okay.

Implied even in positive judgments is an idea of yourself as someone who is limited—someone who needs good things to happen to be okay and feel adequate. There's nothing wrong with something good happening; it's just that even your positive judgments are small truths that are based on a small idea of your self. Your Heart will contract just as much for a small positive truth as for a small negative truth.

Fortunately, there's nothing you need to do about a small truth beyond recognizing it's small. Besides, even small truths can be useful. So there is no need to try to rid yourself of them, which isn't even possible. Seeing that they are small immediately puts them in perspective. Then, when they arise, they are seen as no big deal. You might still think them, but no matter how often they arise, you recognize them as relatively unimportant.

You have probably experienced this ability of a bigger truth to displace or put in perspective a smaller truth. For example, if you or someone you love is suddenly diagnosed with a life-threatening disease, what really matters becomes obvious. The truth, or reality, of a possible death makes many other truths appear small and insignificant in comparison.

You don't need to wait for a big truth to hit you over the head to put your experience in perspective. Simply notice how true each thought is. Experiences come in all different sizes. You are always moving in and out of different degrees of truth, and you are naturally able to discriminate how true each one is. You can determine how truly important something is just by noticing the content of your thought and the sense of self it results in. If it opens and relaxes the sense of your self, your Heart, then it is truly important. If it contracts or limits the sense of your self, your Heart, then it's not.

ALL TRUTH IS RELATIVE

Truth is all there is. Yet our experience of truth, of reality, is always partial. Right now your field of vision is partial. You can only see what is in front of you, not what's behind you. Similarly, your Heart is always showing you the degree of truth of the experience you are having in the moment.

Your view or range of experience is always opening and closing, filling in the blanks in your experience or forgetting or ignoring parts of your experience. Whenever you focus on a particular aspect of experience, you necessarily stop noticing other aspects. As a result, any particular perspective is either smaller and more limited, larger and more complete, or roughly the same degree of completeness as another perspective.

The openness of the sense of your self is always relative. Because truth is always relative, any particular truth could be experienced as an opening or a closing of your Heart. Even a small experience of the truth may be larger than the experience you were just having and therefore will be experienced as an opening or relaxation in your Heart. Similarly, even a fairly large truth can feel limiting if you move into it from an even larger, more spacious experience.

For example, if you've lived most of your life paying attention to your thoughts and ideas, then the first time you are put in touch with your emotions will be experienced as an expansion of consciousness. It will feel like you've discovered a new, rich dimension of your Being.

However, if you've had many even larger experiences of much more expanded states of Being, possibly through spiritual practices, then moving into a strong emotion like anger, sadness, or excitement may be experienced as a contraction or diminishment of the sense of your self. The same truth, the same experience of emotion, can be experienced as either an opening up in your Heart or a closing down. It just depends on where you move into the emotion from and also how open or expanded the sense of your self generally is.

The difference can be slight between two experiences with similar degrees of truth or unimaginably huge. The true dimensions of your Being are limitless. You are everything, and when you directly experience this completeness, the sense of self can be equally vast and limitless.

YOUR PERFECT WISDOM

Your Heart is the wisest thing in the universe. The sense of your self is always perfectly and accurately showing you how true things are, how complete your perspective is in every moment. Even when your Heart is contracted because of some deeply conditioned idea you are holding, it is appropriately and accurately wise in its contraction.

No one has more capacity to distinguish how true things are than anyone else. No one is wiser than you, and no one is less wise than you. Since no one else is able to experience your individual perspective, no one else can ever be more of an expert on your experience than you. Just as someone else can't eat and digest your breakfast for you, others can't experience and digest your perspective of the truth in each moment.

If no Heart is any wiser than any other, perhaps that's because there is just one Heart that functions through many bodies and yet is not contained in any of these particular expressions. What you are is this one Heart of Being.

Since we are all equally endowed with the wisdom of the Heart, there is no need to give away our authority to another. There is nothing better than your own Heart at discriminating how true something is for you right now.

In addition, the thoughts that cause contraction are not your fault. Your thoughts and beliefs were passed on to you by others, who learned them from others. If you trace each conditioned thought or reaction back to its source, you'll discover that all limiting beliefs and ideas are shared among us all. If anyone is to blame for them, it's all of us put together. Another way you could say this is that the whole of Being is the source of everything, even the limited ways we have of experiencing that Being.

With this understanding, the possibility exists to simply trust your Heart, no matter how big or small the truth is that you are experiencing. You can trust your Heart when it opens, and you can trust it when it closes. Your Heart is the wisest and most trustworthy thing there is. In the deepest spiritual traditions, the true teacher, or *satguru,* is seen to be within each of us. Your true teacher is this sensitive and accurate Heart, which expands and contracts as it senses the endless folding and unfolding of life.

APPLYING YOUR HEART'S WISDOM

Because the Heart responds so quickly to what's happening now. . . and now. . . and now, it's helpful to slow down and take your experience one thought or response at a time if you wish to find out how true it is. Just as you can more fully appreciate a meal if you take each bite and savor it, the possibility exists to take time to fully sense a thought that arises.

For example, let's say you remember a disappointing experience and then the thought arises, "My life will never be good enough." Before you rush into thinking of all the ways this is true or, alternatively, defending yourself with reasons why it isn't true, you might take a moment to sense directly how this thought affects the sense of your self. Then, when you know for yourself how true this thought is all by itself, it may be obvious that it is neither completely true nor completely false. If it is sensed directly as a relatively small truth about your life, it may not even be necessary to defend against it with an opposing thought. Sensing how true an initial thought is in this way can reduce the importance of any ensuing thoughts.

Another practical way of exploring and utilizing your Heart's truth-sensing capacity is to check in your Heart when making a choice. By doing that, you can find out what choice is the truer one. However, when it comes to relative choices (e.g., what to do, what to eat, where to live, who to marry, etc.), the differences may be slight in your Heart. From the ultimate perspective, the practical choices we make in life may not be that important. So it may take a while to learn to accurately sense the differences in how true various choices are. But just as a wine connoisseur can learn to discriminate the subtlest difference in flavors, you can learn to sense even very small differences in how true a choice is relative to another.

When checking in your Heart for the truth about some choice, it's helpful to consider as many choices as possible. The truest one may be somewhere in between the possibilities you've considered, or it may be something completely different. For example, a friend was torn between her desire to go permanently on spiritual retreat and her desire to stay with her husband. Neither option felt completely true in her Heart. When I suggested that maybe she could stay with her husband but still go away for long periods of time on spiritual retreats, her Heart opened, as she sensed this was the truest way to respond to both desires.

Exercise: Think of a choice you are considering in your life. It might be best to pick something where you have a decision to make that isn't too important and not too immediate so that you can really explore the process of comparing the truth of your choices. Make a list of possible choices you could make, and be sure to include some that are in between or completely different from the first two options you come up with.

Now really take some time with each choice and sense your Heart's response as you hold in mind the idea of making that choice. Again, keep it simple, and just picture having made the choice, and let go of secondary considerations, such as pros and cons and further ramifications. Notice whether considering a particular choice results in a spacious, easeful sense in your Heart or a contracted sense of your own self. There is no right or wrong way for your Heart to respond. Just notice the way it does respond.

Include the thought that it doesn't matter what you choose. In many cases, the biggest truth about your choices is that what you choose doesn't really matter. If that is the case, then that thought or perspective will give you the most room to just be, and the largest sense of yourself.

Finally, when considering the relative truth of various possible choices, it is also helpful to check in your Heart several times over a period of time. Especially when making major life choices, checking numerous times before acting is more likely to result in a more satisfying outcome. For example, if you want to know if it's true to stay in an intimate relationship, you might find a different result right after an argument than right after your lover has surprised you with a gift. It's a bigger perspective to find out what is truest over the long term than just what is true in the present moment.

The Heart is wise and accurate and can show you how true it is to stay or go, how true it is to buy a house, how true it is to take a new job, even how true it is to eat another cookie. But it also can show you much more of the possibilities inherent in this life and much more of the truth of your Being. In relation to these bigger truths, the practical questions of your life turn out to be relatively small matters. Using your Heart only to know things like what to do or where to live is like using a global positioning satellite system to find your way from your bedroom to your bathroom. It utilizes only a small part of your Heart's capacity.

However, following your Heart day in and day out can put you in touch with the richness of the functioning of this dimension of your Being. Along the way, you may also find your Heart opening in response to the bigger truths and deeper movements of Being that touch every life.

Exercise: For a moment, sense if there is any Peace here. Don't worry how much or if there's only a little bit of Peace here right now. Just notice if you can sense any Peace at all. Now focus your attention on that Peace that is here beneath the flow of thoughts or feelings. Give yourself permission to really sense the nature of Peace and the deep stillness in that experience. As you touch Peace with your awareness, notice if there really is any boundary to the stillness at the core of this moment. Don't worry about doing this right, but just taste as much of the Peace that is here right now as you can.

Now notice the sense of your own Being. Focusing on Peace may have relaxed or opened your sense of self profoundly or just a little. Notice if this has softened or expanded your Heart.

THE MANY SIZES OF TRUTH

The deepest and largest truths don't fit into words or language. While words can act as pointers, your Heart will open the widest and the sense of your self will feel the most complete and full in response to the direct experience of the vast dimensions of Being that are beyond thoughts and beliefs. As always, your own Heart is the truest guide to these larger dimensions and possibilities, but the reason the sense of your self expands when your view of the truth is more complete is because you *are* the truth. You are everything that exists. When you are experiencing more of the truth, you are experiencing more of your self.

The truth comes in many different sizes. One of the primary ways you create and maintain a small sense of self is through a profound involvement with thought. We've been taught from an early age to think, conceptualize, and name things. Because there is such a huge momentum to thinking, moments without a thought happening are rare. Thinking is such a prevalent part of our moment-to-moment experience that many of us live mostly in our minds.

Adding to this momentum of thought are strongly held assumptions and beliefs about the world and yourself, many of which are unconscious. This deeper current of thought also serves to create and maintain a small, separate sense of self. As a result of all of our conscious thinking and unconscious assumptions and beliefs, most people live in awareness of a very small part of reality, most of which only exists in their mind.

This momentum of small truths is reflected in a momentum to your small sense of self. This leads to the question of what to do about it. Unfortunately, any idea about what to do about it is just that—an idea, another thought. However, what *is* possible is to simply be aware of the prevalence of thought in your experience. This awareness is not really something you do, as awareness is a fundamental quality of what you are. Just as you don't need to do anything to have shoulders, you don't need to do anything extra right now to be aware—and to be aware of your thinking.

Exercise: What is thinking like right now? You can notice not only the content of your thoughts, but also the rhythm and speed of your thoughts, the ebb and flow of thought. Where do thoughts come from and where do they go? What happens if there is a pause between thoughts?

How is the sense of your self affected by this flow of thought? Do you need to think in order to be? Does thinking give your sense of self a familiar smallness and sense of boundaries? Is it uncomfortable to not know something in this moment, to not have a thought?

The invitation is to just notice thought and its effect on the sense of your self. Any idea of changing your experience is just another thought that will have a similar effect on the sense of your self. Why not simply find out what thought is like? Experience for yourself how true each thought is. There's nothing wrong with small truths—they're just small. What if all of your thinking is not that big a deal? What if your thinking is just not a very large container for the truth? Thinking can only contain a small amount of the truth.

There is no need to get rid of thought. Once you experience that thought is not a very large container for the truth, this gives way to another question: What else is here besides thought? What else is true? As you sense the prevalence of thought and possibly even the deeper current of unconscious beliefs and assumptions, you may also begin to sense what surrounds and contains thought.

Drop into your Heart and notice the space all around your thoughts. What effect does dropping into your Heart have on your sense of self?

THE DEEPER CURRENTS OF THOUGHT

Many beliefs and assumptions shape and limit our experience of truth and the sense of our self even when we aren't consciously thinking them. They are ideas and concepts that are so deeply believed that they aren't even questioned, such as "Life is short" or "There's never enough time." Furthermore, these beliefs and assumptions generate other thoughts, which add to the momentum of thinking and keep your Heart, the sense of your self, small and contracted.

Two deeper currents of thought strongly shape the experience of your self. The first is the belief in a direction to your life. Usually this direction is toward more, different, or better experiences. But sometimes it's framed in opposite terms as not less, the same, or not worse. In either case, there is a deeply held belief that life should move or change in a particular way.

Of course, things do change, which keeps the hope alive that they will change in the way you want them to. This deeply held assumption that things could or should be better implies a small *you*. The directionality of this assumption is based on a reference point: Things should be better—for *you*. If things should be better for *you*, then *you* must be lacking something. This assumption and the thinking it generates help maintain a small, contracted sense of your self because that is the implied reference point of the assumption—a small *you*.

The second, even deeper and less conscious current of thought that serves to maintain a contracted sense of self is the assumption that physical experience is the most real. This is such a widely held assumption that any other orientation could get you labeled crazy. Even very sensitive and spiritually-oriented people who have had very real and profound experiences of other dimensions are often pulled by this assumption back toward the physical into a more limited experience of truth and their own Being.

There are many dimensions to reality besides the purely physical, and as a human being, your experience includes all of these dimensions. There are the dimensions of thought, emotion, and intuition. And beyond those, are dimensions of pure presence and spacious Being. Many of these dimensions are more real than even physical reality. Experiences of this transcendent reality give you a transcendent sense of your self that is much fuller and more complete than the purely physical sense of your self.

THE THOUGHT THAT YOU ARE THE BODY

The idea that your life could or should be better and the idea that physical reality is the most real animate an even more basic assumption: that you are the body. Your sense of your self, and therefore the experience of your Being, is most often shaped and limited by your identification with the body, which results in the ongoing question, How is it going for the body? Is it better, more pleasurable, or at least not painful right now for the body? This orientation toward the body isn't bad, but it is a limited way of experiencing reality and your self. It's like watching only one channel on your television: It's something, but it's limited.

This limitation can affect every experience you have. By focusing on how it's going for your body, you can miss some of the richest and most profound possibilities in life. The biggest truths may not even be particularly comfortable for your body. Profound states of love and bliss can be exhausting from a purely physical perspective. The deepest realizations of the nature of your Being can be so vast and expansive as to feel like a death for your identity as the body.

Asking what you can do about this limitation will only reinforce it. Another possibility is to explore the sense of limitation that identification with the body gives to your awareness and your Heart.

Exercise: What is it like to believe you are the body right now? Does this allow your Heart to open and relax? Or does it result in a small sense of your self? There is nothing wrong with small truths; they just aren't very complete. You don't have to get rid of or change small truths. Just recognizing they are small is enough.

With the recognition of the incompleteness of identifying with the body, a larger curiosity often arises: What else is true about you? Are you more than the body? What other channels are there on this television called your life? What else is going on here?

THE SENSE OF *ME*

Beneath the assumption that you are the body is an even deeper one. The idea that you are the body is predicated on the assumption that *you* exist, that you are a *me*—a separate, individual self. The most intimate sense of your self is often this sense of *me,* which is a limited and incomplete sensing of your self. It doesn't include the far reaches of your greater Being. This sense of a separate *me* is not bad or wrong; it's just limited and incomplete.

In the midst of a very profound and large experience of truth, the sense of your self can become so large and inclusive that it no longer has much of a sense of being *your* Being. When you awaken to the oneness of all things, the sense of a *me* can thin out quite dramatically. If *you* are the couch you are sitting on, the clouds in the sky, and everything else, then it simply doesn't make sense to call it all *me*. If it is so much more than what you usually take yourself to be, then the term *me* is just too small.

In a profound experience of truth, the sense of *me* softens and expands to such a degree that there is only a slight sense of *me* as a separate self remaining, perhaps just as the observer of the vastness of truth. Beyond these profound experiences of the truth, is the truth itself. When you are in touch with the ultimate truth and the most complete sense of Being, there is nothing separate remaining to sense itself—there is no experience and no experiencer, no Heart, and no sense of self. There is only Being.

The experience of bigger truths and even the biggest truth doesn't obliterate your capacity to experience a small truth and therefore a separate self. But with many experiences of shifting in and out of a small sense of self, this separate self feels more like a suit of clothes you can take on and off than like something permanent. As you move in and out of many dimensions of Being and even beyond experience itself, the boundaries between all of these dimensions become very permeable and inconsequential. It turns out that these boundaries are just thoughts anyway. They don't actually separate anything.

The question isn't how to get rid of a small sense of self, but what is the sense of your self like? Is it fixed or is it constantly shifting—opening and closing, expanding and contracting, tightening and loosening, and sometimes even disappearing altogether? The sense of a separate self can therefore be loosely held even though it continues to contract appropriately when a small truth is triggered.

What is your sense of self like right now? What is true right now? Your Heart is the only guide you need for exploring even the biggest truths.

THERE IS ONLY LOVE

Anything you or anyone else has ever done has been the movement of love. What shapes the movement of love is the sense of *me*. What we are always doing is taking care of the self, whether it is a small sense of self or a more expanded one. Whenever that sense of self is contracted and small, we take care of that *me*. And when it's expanded, we take care of that larger sense of self. All we have ever done is tried to take care of the self in the best way we know how, which is always a loving act.

But, of course, when our actions only take care of a contracted *me*, they don't take care of or take into account other things. For example, we might take care of our taste buds by eating tasty foods, while ignoring our body's need for nutrition. Or if we are so identified with a feeling that all we can do is take care of it, we may not be taking care of our whole Being. Taking care of only the taste buds or only the emotions is still a loving act, but because it is such a narrow way of loving ourselves, it can be neglectful or even harmful to other aspects of our Being or to others.

If we see love in everything we may be afraid that we will allow rape, murder, and other horribly narrow ways of taking care of a small separate sense of *me* to continue. Yet in discovering that there is only love, the surprising thing is that our actions naturally become more loving. If we see murder as an evil that needs to be abolished without also seeing its basic loving nature, that is when it makes sense to murder. If murder is really bad, then it makes sense to kill someone who has murdered someone else. Or it even makes sense to kill someone before they kill us. It makes sense to bomb a country before it attacks us. But when we see the loving nature even of murder, we can respond to it in a way that doesn't perpetuate it, even as we work to prevent it.

It is possible to recognize the love that is already inside of us and already acting through all of us. It is in recognizing that love that the possibility exists for even greater recognition of love. Contrarily, when we reject any aspect of love—which includes anything that's happening—the more contracted our experience will be and the less completely loving our actions will be. So in condemning, we actually become more like what we condemn. Seeing the beauty, perfection, and love within something is what allows it to transform, to move into a more complete way of loving.

When the sense of our self expands, our actions aren't really any more loving; they're just more loving toward a more complete view of the self. When our loving actions take care of a larger sense of ourselves, we appear more saint-like because they are taking into account everybody, since we recognize that we *are* everybody. These actions are still self-gratifying, but they are gratifying to a much broader sense of self.

When the awareness of self becomes even more complete, you come to see that there is ultimately nothing that needs to be changed or fixed. Everything is already fine. The world already is full of love. Your actions and everyone else's are already loving. Whatever Being is doing is Being taking care of itself. That is all it ever does or ever has done.

This leads to an appreciation of everything you do and everything that happens, an appreciation of the way Being moves every time it moves. Love is pouring out everywhere. There's no evidence of the lack of love. What a surprise to discover this in a world that seems so full of problems and things that need to be changed.

TRUE FREEDOM

In this culture where more is felt to be better, there is often an implication that bigger truths are better. If your Heart can open and expand, then it may seem best to find a way to open the darn thing all the way and keep it that way.

However, if you check in your Heart right now as you hold the idea that it's better to open your Heart and keep it that way, you may be surprised to find that this idea actually feels tight or limiting. It's simply not the biggest truth or the most freeing possibility. An even bigger, freer possibility is to allow the sense of your self to be whatever size it is. If your Heart is always accurately and appropriately opening or contracting to show you how true each moment's perspective is, then the best result of experiencing a small truth is for your Heart to contract and show you how small that truth is. It can be as liberating to find out that a small truth is small as to find out that a vast dimension of Being is profoundly real. In both cases, the nature of truth has been more fully illuminated.

Once you realize you can trust your Heart just the way it is right now, whether it is open or closed, you can just rest within the folding and unfolding of all perspectives. You don't do anything to get rid of the small perspectives, which just arise out of the conditioned parts of your Being, and you don't do anything to bring on the bigger perspectives, which just arise out of the unconditioned parts of your Being. You just rest in the moment as it is.

There is never a need to have a bigger or smaller experience, as Being is still Being even in the small experiences. Its nature is the same, and part of its nature is this capacity to discriminate how true—how complete—a particular perspective is. The small experiences of Being are still an expression of Being's ultimate nature, just as a single drop of water is still wet.

Spiritual seekers often think of liberation as staying in an expanded experience of truth. While expanded experiences are freeing (especially when you've been contracted for a long time), the ability to move in and out of many different perspectives is an even greater freedom. Walls are only a problem when you don't know where the door is and therefore can't get in or out.

True freedom is when you can move in and out of identification with a small sense of your self. You don't have to take my word for it. Find out what happens in your Heart if you just let the opening and closing of your sense of self be just the way it is right now. Does this allow your Heart to open? Does it allow you to just be for a moment?

WHO ARE YOU?

What is this Being that you are always sensing to some degree? Perhaps the most surprising discovery is that the sense of your self is not showing you anything about your true nature. A limited sense of your self is never about who you really are! It's not indicative of who you are but, rather, shows you how true your conditioning is. Recognizing this can turn your world inside out. The sense of your self is being shaped and limited by the unfolding of conditioned beliefs and ideas; it's not a reflection of your true nature.

This can be a tremendous relief. All of your experiences of limitation, incompleteness, contraction, insufficiency, or unworthiness have nothing to do with you! Instead, they are accurate reflections of the limitations, incompleteness, smallness, insufficiency, and unworthiness of your ideas, judgments, beliefs, concepts, fears, doubts, worries, hopes, dreams, and desires. They have nothing to do with the nature of you.

The most intimate experience of your self—your Heart—is ultimately never a *complete* experience of your true self. It is always a *relative* experience of the functioning of that true self as it determines the *relative* degree of truth in the particular content of your experience.

This brings us back to the question: Who or what is the Being that you are always sensing to a greater or lesser degree? This question points to what is completely beyond words—and even beyond experience. Even the most expanded *experience* of Being is still not free of this shaping or limitation. In this case the question itself points to a bigger truth than any answer, even an experiential one.

What happens in your Heart when you simply hold the question, Who am I or what am I? Even if your Heart is open, you can still wonder who or what is experiencing the openness. The ultimate truth will never be captured in an experience because it's simply too big to fit in even the most expanded experience. This provides a clue to the question, Who are you? The reason an expanded sense of your self never quite contains the *whole* truth of your Being is that you *are* everything that exists.

Perhaps you can rest now from the dream of experiencing the ultimate truth. The truth is not dependent in any way on your experience of it. It is and always has been functioning just fine through what you call your experience of a self, without ever being contained in that experience. The sense of your self, whether it is expanded or contracted, is a functioning expression of a much larger Being that can never be fully captured in experience.

Perhaps the *experience* of truth doesn't need to be captured. Truth is something we can also unfold gradually bit by bit like a meal or novel that we slowly savor rather than rush through. We are and always have been realizing the truth even when we experience only a small part of it. The richness of Being is also revealed in the small truths that make up our lives.

Being is never harmed by the limited perspectives we experience. Being is not dependent on any particular way of sensing your self, nor even on the absence of a sense of self. Being is already resting within the endless opening and closing of your Heart, so you might as well enjoy the ride.

> *the truth catches up with me*
> *I am not enough*
> *never have been*
> *never will be*
> *what relief to admit this finite container*
> *can never contain infinity*
> *what joy to find infinity*
>   *needs no container*

PART 3

Love Is for Giving, Not for Getting

Love Is for Giving, Not for Getting

What is love and where is it found? We search for love and try to get love, and yet it seems like we never get enough. Even when we've found it, it can slip away as time passes. What if there is a source of love that never fades and is always available? What if love is as near and easy as breathing? What if you have been "looking for love in all the wrong places" instead of actually lacking love?

Love is both simpler and more mysterious and subtle than we imagine it to be. Love is simply the spacious, open attention of our awareness, which is the gentlest, kindest, and most intimate force in the world. It touches things without impinging on them. It holds all of our experience but doesn't hold it down or hold it back. And yet, inherent in awareness is a pull to connect and even merge with the object of your awareness.

It's this seemingly contradictory nature of awareness—the completely open and allowing nature of it and its passionate pull to blend with and even become the object of its attention—that gives life its depth and sweetness. There is nothing more satisfying than this delicious dilemma of being both apart from and, at the same time, connected to something you see, hear, or feel.

Awareness is the beginning of all separation. Prior to awareness, there is just oneness or "is-ness," with nothing separate from the oneness that would be able to experience it. With the birth of awareness comes the subtle distinction of two things: that which is aware and the object of awareness. And yet, those two are connected by this mysterious force we are calling awareness, or love.

This flow of awareness and love that connects you to all you experience is the true source of satisfaction and joy. We have all experienced it to some degree. Whenever you fall in love with a person, pet, piece of music, beautiful object, or anything else, you have felt this flow of intimate, connected awareness. Unfortunately, we've been taught to believe that the source of this good feeling was the object of our affection. So we suffered whenever we lost our apparent source. When your lover leaves, your beloved pet dies, the concert ends, or your dream home is repossessed, you feel bereft of that loving, connected feeling.

YOU ARE THE SOURCE

But what if you are the source of the awareness that connects you to everything? What if the love you have been seeking has always been right here inside your own Heart? What if it doesn't matter what your awareness touches, but only that awareness is flowing? That would profoundly simplify the search for love. Anything or any experience would be a suitable object for your love.

The sweetness of love is in the flow of awareness itself. The completely allowing openness and freedom you might look for from a perfect lover is already here in your own awareness. It doesn't have to try to be accepting because awareness is, by nature, open and allowing. By itself, awareness can't do anything but touch. It can't push or pull or demand something from or limit the freedom of what it touches. And yet, it is not an aloof, distant observer. It is deeply and intimately connected to the object of awareness. In fact, awareness and the object of awareness come from the same source and are ultimately the same thing.

This connection and intimacy that is natural in awareness is satisfying and fulfilling regardless of the object of awareness. In other words, whatever you are experiencing right now is your true love. Whatever you are experiencing is an opportunity to also experience the depth of your true nature as open, loving awareness. Your true nature is true love. It is the perfect lover you have been seeking, and not only is it always here, but it is who you really are.

You might be thinking, "But wait, I don't feel like I'm in love or loving all the time. Sometimes I feel lonely or angry and cut off from love and satisfaction." So how can it be that love is here, but you don't feel it? Is love really absent in those moments, or is it just limited in its expression and flow? Are there really moments when there is no awareness? Or is there always some awareness, even if it isn't a lot? If there were no awareness, there also would be no problems because awareness is the beginning of separation (the sense of a separate self), and the end of awareness is the end of separation. Practically speaking, without awareness, there can't be loneliness, anger, or anything else. So when you are lonely or angry, there is at least some awareness, although possibly not much.

Even when awareness is contracted and tight, as it often is when you are lonely, angry, sad, hurt, or afraid, it has the same nature as when you are happy and excited. Even a single drop of water is still wet, and even a single drop of awareness is still open and allowing of whatever it is touching.

The only trick to experiencing the open and allowing nature of awareness is to look for it in the actual experience you are having. When your awareness is contracted by judgment or fear, it's not actually touching the object of your judgment or fear. Instead, it is touching the judgmental or fearful thought you are having. Awareness is completely allowing and open to that thought. That is the definition of awareness: it is the open and allowing recognition of the content of our experience. If awareness is not open to something, then we are not aware of it.

The key to experiencing love is to notice where awareness is flowing right now. That flow of awareness is love, and it's the most satisfying and nourishing thing you can experience. There is naturally a direction to this flow of awareness. It moves from within your being to the objects nearby and the experiences you are having. You can only fully experience this flow of aware love as it moves in that direction.

When someone else is lovingly aware of you (not of their judgments or desires regarding you, but simply of you as you are), you can experience the outer expression of their love. You can see the way they are looking at you, the smile on their face, and their reactions to you. But the awareness of you is arising in them. The love is flowing from them toward you, and so it is filling them with a sense of satisfaction and joy. If you also are to feel satisfaction and joy, it will depend on whether you are experiencing a flow of love toward them. It is your own open awareness that fills you with that sense of connection and appreciation. *You are filled with love when you are giving it to someone or something else.*

Obviously, it's easier to open your Heart and express love when the requirements of your conditioning are being met. When someone who matches your ideal for a lover is attracted to and interested in you, it's especially easy to give him or her the same openness and attention in return. So naturally, when two people are falling in love, they are both feeling the fullness and richness of the free flow of awareness, or love. But the contact each of them has with that love is within themselves. It's their own love and awareness that is filling them up so richly.

This truth—that you are filled with love when you love, rather than when you are loved—can free you from the search for love outside yourself. If you still aren't sure that it is your own love that fills you, think of a time when someone was in love with you, but you weren't in love with him or her. The flow of loving attention toward you wasn't satisfying. In fact, it might have been uncomfortable having someone so interested in you when you weren't feeling the same way.

In contrast, when you are falling in love with someone, it can be rich, exciting, and energizing, even if it isn't reciprocated. In unrequited love, there is an intensity and beauty from the outward flow of love that is filling you in that moment. So despite the disappointment and hurt of not being loved back, you experience a fullness and aliveness as a result of loving the other. In the Renaissance, unrequited love was even seen as an ideal. It's the love flowing out from your own Heart that fills you with joy and satisfaction. The source is within you.

JUST ONE BEING

There is just one awareness and one Being behind all the individual awarenesses. The way you can reach that oneness of

Being is by experiencing the flow of love from within your being. Paradoxically, the place where you are connected to others is inside your own Heart. You can't really connect to another externally. Even if you used super glue to attach yourself to another person, there would still be a sense of separation in your outer experience, not to mention how hard it might be to disconnect!

On the inside, you are already connected to everyone and everything. The connection is this flow of awareness that is here right now reading these words. It is in the loving nature of awareness that the sense of connection is found, not in the objects of awareness. You are connected to others in the awareness flowing from within you to them. Connection is not found in the flow of awareness and love toward you, as that flow is connected to its source inside the other person.

This is good news! You can experience limitless love no matter what anyone else is doing. The only thing that matters is how much you are loving, not how much you are loved. Right now, you can be filled to overflowing with the incredible sweetness of love, just by giving awareness to anything and everything that is present in your experience. Don't take my word for it; test it out with this exercise:

Exercise: *Allow your awareness to settle on a physical object nearby. Take an extra moment to allow your awareness to fully touch the object. Just for the sake of this* *experiment, give as much love, appreciation, and acceptance as you can to that object. Then notice another object. As your awareness rests for a moment on that, give it as much love, appreciation, and acceptance as you can.*

Now allow your awareness to notice a sound in your environment. As you listen, give that same loving appreciation to the sound you are hearing.

If you have any difficulty giving love and appreciation to a particular object or sound, try another object or sound. If you pick a more neutral object or sound, it will be easier at first to experience loving something for no particular reason.

Continue allowing your awareness to land on various objects, sounds, colors, tastes, smells, and sensations. With each one, allow as much love and appreciation to flow toward it as you can. Take as long as you like with each experience, and if it's difficult to feel love toward something, just move on. It will get easier to love for no reason as you repeat this exercise.

Now notice other things that may be arising within you: an uncomfortable sensation, a thought, a feeling, or a desire. Take an extra moment to send loving attention toward it. Just for now, you can love each sensation, thought, feeling, or desire that appears within you.

As you get the hang of this, you can just allow your awareness to move naturally to whatever it touches next, either inside or outside of you. Whatever it lands on, give it love and acceptance. Just for a moment, let it be the way it is.

What is it like to give simple awareness and love over and over to things that appear in your experience? How open and full does your Heart feel when you are able to give love in this way? If you come to something that's difficult to love or accept, just notice that it's difficult, and then love that it's difficult right now. You can even take a moment to simply love the way some things are harder to love than others. Then move on to whatever is in awareness next.

Just go ahead and love whatever is in front of you, and in that way be filled with love. It's that simple, if you remember that the essence of love is awareness and space. The ideal lover is someone who gives you lots of space to just be yourself but still connects with you as you are. Awareness is like that. It doesn't limit the object of its awareness, but it makes contact.

YOU CAN'T RUN OUT OF LOVE

You can give this awareness or love freely because awareness is the one thing you can never run out of. No matter how many things you've been aware of today, you still have awareness left for this moment and the next. Awareness is easy to give, and it doesn't cost anything or deplete you in any way. In your

Heart, there is a limitless supply of love. Just see if you can give so much attention to something that you end up with no more awareness.

We sometimes withhold love and awareness because we think that true love requires more than this simple, open attention. Our conditioning suggests that love requires things like compromise, sacrifice, and unconditional giving of our time and effort. Perhaps some of these are necessary for a relationship, but not for love.

This is an important distinction, as we often confuse love and relationship. We mistakenly believe that love is dependent on relationship. But if we recognize that the source of love is within us, then relationship can be seen in perspective. Relationships are important, but they aren't as important as love. The experience of this inner flow of love is satisfying, either with or without a relationship. You can experience it with a beautiful object of art in a museum, a moving piece of music, an exciting moment in a sporting activity, or in a deep connection with another person. Love is what makes relationships and everything else worthwhile.

What a rich possibility—that all the love you have ever wanted is available right now, just by giving it to everything you encounter, both within you and in the environment. Love is for giving, not for getting. And the more you give, the more fully it fills your Heart to overflowing.

LOVING THROUGH THE SENSES

We are filled with love when we give it away, not when we receive it from others. This truth can profoundly free you from the search for love, as anything is a worthy object of your love. Especially when you realize that love is simply awareness and space, you can freely give it to everything that appears in your experience. In this way, you are filled to overflowing with the sweet open presence of love.

It is also possible to experience this fullness of love through your physical senses. For the most part, we use our senses to *take things in:* We look at something to get something, such as information. We might look in our wallet to see how much money we have left. Or we look in the fridge to see what there is to eat. We listen to the radio for some entertainment or news. We feel our pocket to see if our car keys are in there.

Or we might try to get something more than information through our senses: We watch carefully to try to feel safe. We stare longingly at a photo of someone to try to be filled with love or to be satisfied by their beauty. We listen to music to try to be filled with excitement or joy. In a sense we have learned to be consumers with our senses. We try to acquire beauty, pleasure, excitement, passion, happiness, security, value and even love by ingesting these through our senses. But just as love from the outside doesn't ever fill us up or completely satisfy us, anything we try to consume with our senses isn't ultimately satisfying.

Unfortunately, the experiences we take in through our senses do satisfy a little. Looking at a beautiful woman or man does give us a little bit of pleasure, excitement, and the experience of beauty. However, such pleasure and excitement are very fleeting and never enough. This is actually an unavoidable part of the nature of life and of our Being. The truth of our Being is pure emptiness or space. So when we take in any experience, it flows into the inner emptiness of our Being and, in the process, is dissolved by that emptiness. The inward flow of experience is a flow from form to emptiness. Everything we consume with our senses and awareness returns to its original nature as formless presence.

This is why the satisfaction we get from outer experience is never enough. Trying to fill ourselves up with beauty, passion, happiness, and love from the outside is like trying to fill a leaky bucket. No matter how long you stand there with the hose pouring water into that bucket, it never fills up. No matter how many experiences of passion, beauty, and joy you consume, the inner emptiness of your Being is still totally empty. And no matter how much love or attention you receive from others, it's never enough to fill the hole in your heart. You can never get enough of what doesn't satisfy.

Because of this, our attempts to feel good by ingesting or consuming outer experiences can lead to a compulsive or an addictive attachment to outer experiences, including fun, beauty, or romance. A basic principle of psychology is that an intermittent reward is more powerfully reinforcing than a constant one. So the little taste of excitement or satisfaction we do experience from seeing a beautiful person, tasting chocolate, or traveling to Fiji can lead to a slight, or even severe, addiction to the outer experience. People can become addicted to just about anything, including scanning the crowd for a beautiful face or planning ways to maximize fun or pleasure. This can also result in avoidance of or overreaction to things we don't want to experience: We may tighten or withdraw when we see the wrinkles in our lover's face, or we may not eat the healthiest foods if we don't want to taste them.

Fortunately, there is a simple solution. It is in the outward flow of the positive qualities of our Being, including love, that we can fully experience the peace, joy, love, and beauty within us. When joy, peace, or excitement is flowing from within us, it is moving from emptiness to form. The inner emptiness of Being is the source of everything, including joy, passion, peace, strength, compassion, support, and love. So it is in the outward flow of awareness and love that we are filled with the experience of these qualities. It's in this movement from emptiness to form that these particular qualities take shape. Emptiness moves into the particular forms of love, peace, joy, and everything else with the outward flow of awareness.

Surprisingly, the inner empty source never runs out. There's always more joy and love to be found in their true source.

Because of the habit of trying to consume things with our senses, instead of feeling this fullness of Being, we often feel empty, hungry, and incomplete. So we go looking, listening, and feeling for something else to satisfy us. We may compulsively look for a better lover, a better car, or a better job even when the lover, car, or job we have is actually quite wonderful. We may develop the habit in the way we watch or listen to the world of always looking for something to take in with our senses that will satisfy us. Of course, many people experience this when it comes to food. We want joy and satisfaction by tasting something, and yet we can never eat enough. Similarly, we want joy and satisfaction from seeing or hearing something of beauty, but we can never see or hear enough to satisfy. Audiophiles are forever searching for a better sounding set of speakers.

There is another way: We can *give* love through our senses. Instead of trying to see or take in something exciting or satisfying with our eyes, we can shower whatever is in our sight with a flow of love through our eyes. This is as easy as shifting the focus to the outward flow of awareness rather than the inward flow of sensation.

Exercise: Take a moment to look at something in your environment. Start with something neutral or something you find pleasing to the eye. Notice how you are relating inwardly to the experience of sight. Are you trying to get something from looking? Is there an evaluation of what you are looking at? Is it good enough? Is it satisfying enough right now to simply look at this object?

Now allow a fuller flow of awareness through your eyes to the object. Instead of trying to take in the object through your eyes, shower it with a fullness of loving attention through your eyes. Just for a moment, love it for no reason with your seeing. Love is ultimately acceptance and attention, so just give the object lots of attention and acceptance. Notice if you can feel a sense of love flowing out of your eyes to the object. Use your sight to give love to the object instead of to get something from it.

What is that like to feel an outward flow of love through your eyes? Don't worry if you are doing it right or if you are feeling it enough. Just notice how it shifts your experience to whatever degree it does, or just imagine a flow of love through your sense of sight to the object.

Now pick another object and, once again, allow loving awareness to flow out of your eyes to the object. Just for now, allow as much love as you can to flow through seeing to the object. Now move from object to object and shower each of them with love, just for the sake of this experiment. As you get the hang of it, you can even try it with objects you don't like or even strongly dislike. You can also try it with people and pets. Notice how some things are easier to look at this way than others, but give as much love to each thing as you can.

You can repeat this experiment with your other senses. What would it be like to shower things with love through your hearing? Your sense of touch? Your taste buds? What if the most important thing isn't how good your food tastes, but how much you love it with your mouth? We started with the sense of sight, as that sense has the greatest quality of separation or distance to it. Hearing, touch, and taste are just naturally more intimate senses, while seeing entails more of an experience of separation. However, that sense of separation can be profoundly shifted to a feeling of connectedness by giving love to things through your eyes. Here is a similar exercise for the sense of touch.

Exercise: Take a moment to touch something with your hands. Start with something neutral or something you find pleasing to touch, like a soft pillow or blanket. Notice how you are relating inwardly to the experience of touching. Are you trying to get something from the sensations in your hands? Is it satisfying enough to simply touch this object? Notice the inherent intimacy in touching something. There's no distance between you and the object you are touching. Is there really any separation right now as you touch it?

Now allow a fuller outward flow of awareness through your hands to the object. Instead of trying to take in the feel of the object, shower it with a fullness of loving attention through your hands. Just for a moment, love it for no reason with your touch. Love is ultimately acceptance and attention, so just give the object lots of attention and acceptance. Notice if you can feel a sense of love and acceptance flowing out of your hands to the object. Use your hands and the sense of touch to give love to the object instead of to get something from it.

How is it to feel an outward flow of love through your hands? Don't worry if you are doing it right or if you are feeling it enough. Just notice how it shifts your experience to whatever degree it does that, or just imagine a flow of love through your sense of touch to the object.

Now touch another object and, once again, allow loving awareness to flow out of your hands to the object. Just for now, allow as much love as you can to flow through your hands to the object. Now move from object to object and shower each of them with love, just for the sake of this experiment. As you get the hang of it, you can try this with objects you don't like to touch or even strongly dislike. You can also try it with people and pets. Notice how some things are easier to touch this way than others, but give as much love to each thing as you can.

Now include the internal sensations of your own body. In a very intimate way, you are touching everything inside of you. Your kinesthetic sense of touch includes being able to feel the joints, muscles, and even the organs of your body. Notice what happens if you give loving acceptance and attention to your arms and legs in the same way you did to the physical objects around you. Just for now, fully feel any sensation that arises in your body and directly send love and awareness to it.

Repeat the above exercise and substitute the sensation of hearing. Explore the experience of loving things through your ears. And then try it with the sense of smell and taste at your next snack or meal. Because these other senses are more intimate than the sense of sight, you may discover that it is very satisfying and rich to give love in these more immediate and intimate ways. You can also combine all your physical senses and love the totality of your present moment sensory experience:

Exercise: Take a moment to love something through one of your senses. Notice if you are trying to get something from the sensation. Now allow a fuller outward flow of awareness through your sensing to the object. Shower the object with a fullness of loving attention. Just for a moment, love it for no reason.

Now notice another sensation and allow love and acceptance to flow to another sight, sound, smell, taste, or tactile sensation. And then love another sensation and another and so on. Be sure to include the sensations of your own body, including whatever is happening inside of you and whatever you can experience of your own body through sight, listening, and touch.

How is it to feel an outward flow of love through all your senses? Don't worry if you are doing it right or if you are feeling it enough. Just notice how it shifts your experience to whatever degree it does, or just imagine a flow of love through all of your senses to your present moment experiences.

Now allow awareness and spaciousness to flow to all your sensory experience at once. Include every sensation you are having, and notice that you can love them all at the same time. The source of awareness is limitless, and you can't run out of awareness and love, so why not give as much awareness and love as you can to everything that's here right now? Don't worry if you are including everything or not. Just allow your awareness to flow out in as many directions and to as many sensations as you can. What is it like to just love the totality of your sensations?

LOVING BEYOND THE SENSES

You can include more subtle sensations if you experience these, but being able to experience subtle energies and dimensions isn't necessary to experiencing the fullness of love. Thoughts, emotions, and desires are also a more subtle level of experience than physical sensations.

> *Exercise: Take a moment to love something through one of your senses. Now allow a fuller outward flow of awareness through your sensing to the object. Shower it with a fullness of loving attention. Notice another sensation and allow love and acceptance to flow to another sight, sound, smell, taste, or tactile sensation. Then love another sensation and another and so on. Allow awareness and spaciousness to flow out of all your senses at once. Include every physical sensation you are having, and notice that you can love them all at the same time.*
>
> *Now notice any thoughts or emotions that are arising, and allow this same loving attention to flow to them as well. If a strong desire or longing arises, include it in the total flow of open awareness. And if you sense any energy or presence in the room, love it for no reason as well. Don't be concerned if you don't sense anything beyond the physical, as it really doesn't matter. Just love whatever you are experiencing in this moment. It is satisfying to love anything*

and everything, so why leave anything that is here right now out of this abundant flow of sensing and awareness? What is it like to include everything in your loving flow of awareness?

You can even love whatever you are not experiencing in this moment. You can love through your physical senses, through pure awareness, and through sensing existence itself. In this way, you can love the entire universe and beyond. It is rich to love what's here in your direct experience, and you can also simultaneously love what lies beyond your immediate sensory experience. Just send love to everything even if you can't see it or feel it. What is it like to simply give more and more love?

There is one more place you can send love, and that is to all time:

Exercise: Love whatever you are experiencing in this moment. Include everything in your loving flow of awareness: everything you can see, hear, touch, feel, and everything you can't. Let love flow to the infinite reaches of space throughout the universe and beyond.

You can also send love through this present moment in time to every other moment in time. Start by loving the exquisite immediacy of the experience you are having in this moment, and then send love to every memory or thought about the future that arises in the immediacy of this present moment. Now also send love to the past and future, to the endless array of intensely immediate "nows" that have ever appeared and that will ever appear. Don't worry if you are doing it right. Just send love, and let the love find its own way to the past and future. Notice what it's like to love the entire flow of time. Include as much of eternity as you can.

Notice what your experience of the present moment is like when you allow limitless love and acceptance to flow out of this moment to every other moment in time. Does loving all the moments of your life and beyond limit or restrict your experience of this moment? Or does loving all of time allow you to even more fully experience and love the precious uniqueness of this very instant? Paradoxically, loving all time can bring us into even more intimate contact with the present moment.

You don't need to pick and choose what to love. Anything will do, from a dryness in your mouth, to the feel of a dog's fur, to the sound of the wind, to the mystery of thought, to the infinity of space itself, or even to a direct mystical sensing of something beyond your normal senses, such as the infinite expanse of time itself.

The wonderful thing about being filled with love and joy from showering simple awareness and love on whatever appears in our experience is that it frees us from having to find or get the right experiences or from having to avoid the wrong ones. If you can be filled to overflowing with the sweetness of love by looking at a plastic wastebasket in this way, consider how that might affect your Saturday night dates! While you don't have to marry the first person you shower with love through your eyes, you may discover that physical appearance isn't as important to love and romance as you thought. Similarly, it might not matter as much as you thought what song is playing on the radio, what is being served for dinner, whether you are having an expanded or contracted experience, whether you are suffering or not, or what is happening period. If everything is a potential object for this limitless flow of love, then you can just relax and love whatever is in front of you or whatever is happening right now.

LOVE REVEALS INNER BEAUTY

There is an even more surprising discovery you may make: When you shower something with love, it reveals its inner beauty. Just as a black light reveals the fluorescence in a poster from the sixties, the love in your awareness can reveal the beauty, value, wonder, and intrinsic worth and perfection that is in everything. The secret to experiencing more perfection in the world isn't to create a flawless life full of exquisite objects of art, beautiful lovers, delicious food, and exclusively pleasurable experiences, but to shower every object, every person, and every experience with the inner fullness of love until its inner beauty shines with a profound radiance. You can do this in a fantastic mansion or at the local garbage dump. You can do this with a beautiful movie star or with the grouchy old man who lives on your street.

You can also do this with your own body and personality. This love that flows through your senses is actually what you are. The body and personality that you experience yourself as are really just more objects to love. All the reactions, thoughts, desires, and inner sensations that arise within you are simply more things to love. They are as beautiful as everything else.

There is also intense and vast beauty, perfection, and wonder within the larger dimensions of your Being. Empty space reveals a glorious texture, fullness, and softness beyond the softest thing in the universe when you love it fully and without reservation. Time becomes an infinite playground of possibility and creation when you love it with all your heart. Presence and all the qualities of your being, including love, peace, joy, clarity, and strength are the most delicious flavors you can imagine when you just love them with all your senses and with awareness itself.

Don't take my word for any of this. Find out for yourself what happens when you love for no reason, especially if you include anything and everything. Love is for giving and giving, and then giving some more.

BEYOND THE EXPERIENCE OF LOVE

Beyond the possibility of experiencing more and more love in your Heart, is the even richer discovery that love is what you are, and what you have always been. This open flow of awareness is what you are made of. It is your true nature. When you are experiencing more love, you are experiencing more of your true self.

The recognition that love is your essence, your nature, allows an ultimate sense of fullness that isn't dependent even on experiencing love. If love is what you are, then it doesn't matter if you are experiencing it right now or not. If for a moment you don't experience your shoulders, do you lose your shoulders? No, they are part of you and are always here, whether you are noticing them or not. This is not to say that it doesn't matter whether you experience the complete potential for love that exists within you. However, once you have discovered and repeatedly experienced the truly limitless nature of the love that you are, it doesn't matter whether you are experiencing that right now or not because you know that that infinite potential is still who you are and who you will always be.

While it's rich to explore and discover the limitless capacity of your Heart to love, and then love some more, you can also simply rest here as love itself. Love at rest is still love. When love is resting as the pure potential for love, it is just another dimension of its accepting and allowing nature.

Love is not just a part of you; it's the nature, or essence, of every part of you. The capacity for open, spacious awareness is always here, even if you are using only a very small portion of this capacity. All of the exercises and prescriptions in this book are actually descriptions of what has always been true. No matter how much or how little love is flowing in this moment, love is still always here. It's who you are and who you have always been.

Every moment of your entire life has been an experience of the flow of awareness and love to something. Even when love isn't being experienced, there isn't any less love; there is just less of the outward flow or expression. The source is still here in all its glory. Love is not only for giving, it is what you are.

I may think I feel love
but it is love that feels me
constantly testing the woven fibers
that enclose and protect my heart
with a searing flame
that allows no illusion of separation

and as the insubstantial fabric of my inner fortress
is peeled away by the persistent fire
I desperately try to save some charred remains
by escaping into one more dream of passion

I may think I can find love
but it is love that finds me

meanwhile, love becomes patient and lies in wait
its undying embers gently glowing
and even if I now turn and grasp after the source of warmth
I end up cold and empty-handed
I may think I can possess love
but it is love that possesses me

and finally, I am consumed
for love has flared into an engulfing blaze
that takes everything
and gives nothing in return
I may think love destroys me
but it is love that sets me free

ABOUT THE AUTHOR

After a lifetime of spiritual seeking, Nirmala met his teacher, Neelam, a devotee of H.W.L. Poonja (Papaji). She convinced Nirmala that seeking wasn't necessary. And after experiencing a profound spiritual awakening in India in 1998, he began offering satsang with Neelam's blessing. This tradition of spiritual wisdom has been most profoundly disseminated by Ramana Maharshi, a revered Indian saint, who was Papaji's teacher. Nirmala's perspective was also greatly expanded by his friend and teacher, Adyashanti.

Nirmala is also the author of *Nothing Personal: Seeing Beyond the Illusion of a Separate Self* and *Gifts with No Giver,* a book of nondual poetry, and many other writings that are available as free downloads on his website: **www.endless-satsang.com**. In addition to giving satsang throughout the U.S. and Canada, Nirmala is available for Nondual Spiritual Mentoring sessions in person or over the phone. To arrange a session, contact him at nirmalanow@aol.com. Nirmala lives in Sedona, Arizona with his wife, Gina Lake. More information about her and her books is available at **www.radicalhappiness.com**.

Made in the USA
Lexington, KY
24 November 2013